# From Therapy to Life Mastery:
## Coaching as a Natural Next Step from Hypnotherapy

**David Hartman, LCSW, Board Certified Coach**
**& Diane Zimberoff, LMFT, Board Certified Coach**

Ah, mastery... what a profoundly satisfying feeling when one finally gets on top of a new set of skills... and then sees the light under the new door those skills can open, even as another door is closing.

*Gail Sheehy*

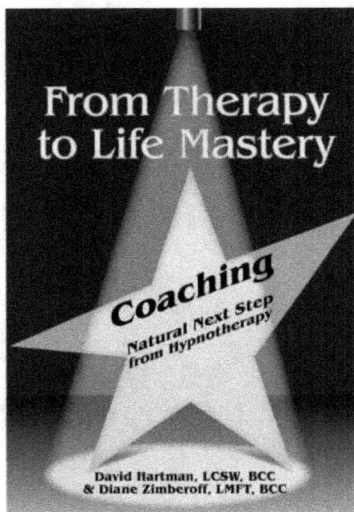

From Therapy to Life Mastery

Coaching
Natural Next Step from Hypnotherapy

David Hartman, LCSW, BCC
& Diane Zimberoff, LMFT, BCC

Published by:

Wellness Press
The Wellness Institute
3716 - 274th Ave SE
Issaquah, WA 98029
800-326-4418
www.wellness-institute.org

ISBN 978-0-9622728-7-5

# Table of Contents

# Index of Processes to Facilitate

# Chapter One
# Introduction to Life Coaching

## David Hartman and Diane Zimberoff*

In this book we will explore the potential benefits of coaching for the professional and for your clients:

- Offer your existing therapy clients a "next step" in their growth work with you, helping them 'to discover their passions and unlock their brilliance'[1]
- Attract a new base of highly motivated clients: expand your target market beyond people who want therapy to those who want mastery
- Place yourself on the cutting edge of the new "positive psychology" movement.

We will elucidate the key qualities of life coaches, and discuss at some length the differences between coaching and therapy. Both approaches overlap in the areas of solving problems, changing habits, handling emotions, accepting accountability, and improving relationships. We will offer clear distinctions between when to teach, when to process, and when to engage in nondirective coaching.

The focus in psychology and psychotherapy for most of the twentieth century was on repairing the negatives of symptoms, traumas, disorders and deficits. Then around the turn of the century a refreshing movement began to gain credibility: Positive psychology and positive psychotherapy. Positive psychotherapy contrasts with standard therapeutic interventions for symptoms of mental or emotional dysfunction by *increasing* positive emotion, engagement, character strengths, and meaning rather than directly targeting negative symptoms.[2] This developing trend is a direct descendent of the humanistic psychology movement and transpersonal psychology which evolved in the second half of the twentieth century. A further

---

* The Wellness Institute, 3716 - 274th Ave SE, Issaquah, WA 98029 ◆ 800-326-4418

development in this continuum has taken hold in many parts of the world today: life coaching. Coaching incorporates the added dimension of adult development for *optimal* functioning.

"There is considerable debate in the literature on the difference between coaching and psychotherapy . . . Although there are differences between coaching and therapy (Gray, 2006; Levinson, 1996), effective coaches move along the continuum between them to deal with the needs of the executive and his/her organization."[3]

In a parallel fusion, effective counselors and therapists move along that same continuum: The American Counseling Association defines counseling as "The application of mental health, psychological, or human development principles, through cognitive, affective, behavioral or systematic intervention strategies, that address wellness, personal growth, or career development, as well as pathology."[4]

Coaching, as its central function, facilitates change and development into as yet unrealized potential.

'Coaching hypnosis' may be referred to as the deliberate use of hypnotic strategies and principles as an adjunct to accepted coaching process. The inclusion of hypnosis, NLP techniques, and hypnotic strategies and principles in coaching is not only appropriate but highly effective. We will document some of the neuroscience reasons for this. One is the increased manufacture of theta brain wave frequencies within the hypnotic trance state, the same state as we experience in REM sleep when we are dreaming.

Hypnosis creates a state of dual effect: relaxation yet responsiveness. The conscious mind is calmed, enabling access to the unconscious mind. Maldonado and Spiegel[5] define this as 'trance logic' – a way of reasoning that does not follow the rules of 'normal' logical processes. Through this mechanism, an individual may have experiences and interpret them in ways that transcend the person's conscious rational belief system, opening new perspectives and expanded horizons of what is possible.

The style of coaching we are advocating tends to be humanistic, developmental, and systemic. It tends, therefore, toward being non-directive, developmental, and therapeutic. Yet it is possible to achieve a balance between the extremes of the foregoing categories, maintaining accountability for performance toward goal achievement.

## The model of sports coaching

Coaching entails identifying steps to take to reach clear objectives, in the way a sports coach works to boost an athlete's performance.[6] Traditionally in sports coaching, to be effective coaches must perform multiple roles, e.g., teacher, motivator, strategist, organizer, character builder (cf. Gould, 1987).[7]

The teaching aspect varies with the level of achievement already accomplished by the coachee. It may well focus more on refining existing skills and perspectives than on teaching new ones. Often, a coach's teaching focuses on discipline, training and conditioning, and organizing effective practice. This in turn requires an effective coach to have keenly perceptive diagnostic skills in order to assess the coachee's talent, strengths and vulnerabilities.

Motivation involves the ability to affect the psychological skills and states of their athletes. One of the specific skills that an effective coach uses to motivate is well-timed and nurturing corrective feedback.

Strategy is the ability to coach during competition and lead their athletes to a successful performance. This entails clear prioritization, recognition of every existing or potential challenge, and honest self-assessment of one's level of preparation, confidence, and mastery of the necessary skills.

Organization is one of the most basic building blocks of the coach's functions. Strategizing and prioritizing and assessment of challenge and resources all require a high degree of organization. And often it is just this innate talent that is missing or underdeveloped by those who are in need of coaching.

Character building involves influencing the personal development of and positive attitude toward sport in their athletes, leading to positive attitudes about sportsmanship and fair play, high levels of self-esteem, respect for others, and robust team cohesion.

## The model of "Stepping into Your Greatness"

Some people no doubt hear grandiosity and egotism in the concept of "Stepping into Your Greatness." Abraham Maslow[8] warned about the self-defeating trap of the "fear of one's own greatness."

Stepping into your greatness means *transcending unnecessary limitation*. We all carry within us deeply imprinted assumptions about what we are capable of, and incapable of. Those assumptions are built around generalizations (early conclusions) of other people's beliefs. As children we accepted as gospel truth what the adults in our lives told us, or communicated to us in nonverbal ways. And those beliefs continue to be a primary influence on our perception of life and of ourselves, limiting the choices we make.

Transcending these limitations calls on our capacity to stand outside of our conditioned perspective, to see the world and ourselves more objectively. With such a viewpoint, one is more open, more accepting, less egotistic. One finds a deeper sense of meaningfulness, purpose, and connection. We see transcendence at work in selfless service or self-sacrificing altruism, in the humble acceptance of the opportunity to use one's natural gifts for the greater good of all.

Ralph Metzner summarized ten classical metaphors of self-transformation, or self-transcendence, in a beautiful article in the *Journal of Transpersonal Psychology* in 1980[9]:

(1)   From dream-sleep to awakening
(2)   From illusion to realization
(3)   From darkness to enlightenment
(4)   From imprisonment to liberation
(5)   From fragmentation to wholeness
(6)   From separation to oneness
(7)   From being on a journey to arriving at the destination
(8)   From being in exile to coming home
(9)   From seed to flowering tree
(10)  From death to rebirth

Let's use the personal transformation tools we all know to awaken from normality, what Abraham Maslow called "a psychopathology of the average, so undramatic and so widely spread that we don't even notice it."[10]

**The role of coaching within the mental health profession**

The focus on goals distinguishes coaching from traditional mental health treatment, which is more concerned with ameliorating personal pathologies.[11] Coaching is also distinct from therapy with regard to the practitioner–client relationship and to the setting in which it is conducted.[12]

A call to action has been raised within the social work profession regarding the role of coaching and its place within the profession's scope of practice. "Social workers must begin to actively talk about the role of coaching in social work, and address the following questions:

- What is the relationship of coaching to social work? Should social work define its scope of practice to include coaching?
- What are the licensing issues? If coaching can be done without licensure, how are best practices ensured and defined?
- What ethical issues need to be resolved? Can social workers engage in coaching without violating the current Code of Ethics?
- When should practitioners operating as coaches identify themselves as social workers?
- What criteria should social workers use to determine whether or not coaching should be used instead of other techniques?"[13]

These same issues apply to psychologists, marriage and family therapists, and licensed professional counselors. For example, the Society of Consulting Psychology, Division 13 of the American Psychological Association, states in its 2005 Guidelines[14]:

> Coaching – Practitioners learn how to provide competent, assessment-anchored coaching and other individual-level interventions. The goals of such activities include helping clients to improve their abilities to diagnose problems that they are confronting in the workplace, to change problematic attitudes, values, beliefs, and behaviors that may interfere with their performance, and to improve their skills, self-awareness, and self-efficacy in their work related roles. Coaching may include education and training interventions as part of a package of activities that are usually negotiated and delivered to a client in the context of a formal agreement.

# Chapter Two
# Components of Life Coaching

## 1. Communication skills

Establishing rapport and trust at the beginning of the relationship is an obvious requirement to proceed further. One reason professionals who are trained therapists make such good coaches is that they have mastered the ability to engender trust from their clients from the beginning. And one of the most important ingredients in doing so is effective listening, with active listening and powerful questioning that challenges the client's assumptions and self-limiting beliefs. The ethical coach is careful to discover the client's intentions and desired outcomes, their preferred style of working and of being challenged. It is vital to keep the coach's beliefs, judgments, perceptions, and intentions from interfering with the client's. This can only create miscommunication, resistance, and false starts. And, of course, it runs counter to the very premise of the desired outcome of coaching in the first place, namely empowerment of the client to realize his/her own potential destiny as it is revealed to him/her.

Two NLP (Neurolinguistic Programming) techniques that are powerfully useful for the coach in the communication with clients are *framing* and *reframing*. These techniques are helpful in both active listening and powerful questioning. Framing is an NLP construct implying a way of perceiving something or setting a context. For example, consider the difference between "Do you want to buy this car?" and "Will you finance this car here or at your bank?" These two questions are addressing the same basic issue, but they are framed differently -- they are presented in different ways and under different assumptions. The first is framed in a more passive, open manner, while the second implies that you <u>are</u> buying the car and the only issue is how you will pay for it. It is all in how a skilled salesperson asks. Now applying the technique to coaching, there is a world of difference between "Do you see your business growing over the coming year?" and "Will your business grow more through adding new customers or repeat sales to existing customers?" Of course, first the client's intention to grow their business must be determined;

otherwise the coach is making an unsupported assumption. However, the wording of the question itself establishes parameters for the client's response.

Reframing is the technique of changing the customary way the client perceives a given situation into a new perspective. The coach might reframe the *context*, i.e., place a "problem" response or behavior in a different context that gives it a new and different, and usually more positive meaning. For example, with a client struggling with a self judgment about being too assertive in business dealings, the coach might offer, "Your aggressiveness toward your competitors is actually useful in your efforts to excel." On the other hand, the coach might reframe the *meaning*, ascribing a new meaning to a behavior or response without changing the context. This is usually done by directing attention to previously deleted aspects; e.g. "You thought she was just slow; you didn't notice how thorough and reliable she is."

"Clean language" is a concept developed by David Grove[15] to facilitate people to identify, develop, explore, and evolve their metaphors using the basic Clean Language questions. The questions are designed for working with the metaphoric and symbolic domain of experience, and were originally devised to help clients resolve deep trauma. Grove's intervention works by first allowing the client to put what they want to change in symbolic form, then creating a safe, interactive area for the symbols, and, finally, once the symbols change, healing begins, with a new experience replacing a suffering one.

In coaching hypnosis we directly access the client's unconscious, and the words he/she uses to communicate their experience are precise and personally deeply meaningful to the client. We always want to use the client's exact words, not substituting "angry" when they say "pissed" or "alone" when they say "lonely". Our language conveys interpretation and suggestion, and we want to avoid either one.

Explicitly introducing Clean Language into one's approach to psychotherapy sharpens the focus on the client's own inherent wisdom. The *less* we attempt to change the client's model of the world, the *more* they experience their own core patterns, and organic, lasting changes naturally emerge. David Grove quite radically modified the traditional philosophy of NLP by using clean language (containing a minimum of presupposition) to replace typical NLP patterns of language which are designed to have *maximum* influence, often through the covert use of suggestion. NLP is based on the notion that you can take an experience, find its structure and if you change its structure it changes the experience. Thus the Clean Language coach *follows* the natural direction of the process rather than *leading* it.

What Grove discovered was the more he used Clean Language, the more clients naturally used metaphor to describe their symptoms. When Clean Language questions were then directed to the metaphors and symbols, unexpected information became available to the client, often with profound results. By interfering with a client's description of their symptoms with interpretation and suggestion, well-meaning coaches can rob clients of the very experience needed to resolve their unwanted behaviors.

Working with symbol and metaphor is the forte of Clean Language. The aim is for the *client* to gather information about their own subjective experience, not necessarily for the *coach* to understand it. Common by-products of being asked Clean Language questions are: a state of self-absorption (trance often spontaneously develops); a sense of connecting with some deep, rarely explored aspects of ourselves; and a sense of wonder, curiosity and awe at the marvelous ingenuity of our unconscious.

When a coach makes even minute changes to a client's words the implications can be significant. Clients often have to go through additional translation processes and mental gymnastics to reorient to the coach's presuppositions. Thus the intervention subtly goes in a direction determined by the coach's map of the world.

To illustrate how easy it is to unwittingly interfere in a client's process, let's explore an example. A coach could respond in a number of ways to the following statement: "I'm stuck with no way out."

It is highly therapeutic to begin by fully validating the client's 'current reality' that there is no way out of stuck through the use of Clean Language. It may be tempting to want to direct the client, subtly or not-so-subtly, toward a solution. But that is short-circuiting the client's exploration of their dilemma.

There are 9 basic Clean Language questions. Two questions request information about attributes and two ask for location information. There are two questions which reference the past and two which reference the future. One question offers the client the opportunity to make a metaphorical shift in perception. The 9 basic Clean Language questions are:

- And is there anything else about ......?
- And what kind of ...... is that ......?
- And where is ......?
- And whereabouts?
- And what happens next?
- And then what happens?
- And what happens just before ......?
- And where does/could ...... come from?
- And that's ...... like what?

One way to conceptualize verbal communication between two people is the following six categories:

- **Sharing** A quick, heartfelt snapshot of who you are. Speak deeply, authentically, comprehensively. The coach listens well, and models honest sharing.
- **Debriefing** A list of what someone has done since the last session, a detailed report. What could you do differently? What worked? Clarification.
- **Clearing** Venting feelings through emotional release. "Getting something off their chest." Listen for the passion behind the emotion: surface the values that may apply on a broader basis.
- **Discussion** and **Debate** Expressing views and opinions. Best and most productive when the shared space allows equal time to everyone. Neither form is used much in coaching. Rather, coaches encourage **dialogue**: flowing with ideas without taking a stand, listening with intuition, allowing for silences.
- **Teaching** "I know something that you may not know, and I would like to share it with you." Coaches should be cautious with teaching, because it undermines partnership. Teaching is appropriate in small doses.
- **Coaching** Unlike the other forms of conversation, coaching prompts people to generate their next new

action. People explore what they want in the future and choose ways to obtain it – without getting advice. Involves exploring, problem solving, creative thinking, generating multiple options (including contradictory ones), and experimenting with new strategies and techniques. What keeps the client awake at night, and what is their highest aspiration?

## 2.  Motivation

Motivating clients to make tough choices and implement changes in their traditional way of doing things is one of a coach's primary responsibilities. That motivation must come from their own core personal values (what is most important) and core personal strengths (what they do well and are building on). Here the coach's listening skills pay dividends, because he/she will know what the client's values are. What is so important that the individual is willing to really sacrifice to get it? And, setting modesty or pride aside, what is a realistic assessment of strengths that are available, or can be refined, to achieve the desired result? Overestimating one's abilities is as destructive as underestimating them.

This self-assessment, kept honest and accurate by the coach's objectivity, also identifies areas that otherwise remain obscured and unexamined in the shadows. What are the client's dominant shadows? The coach's involvement must address any areas of self-sabotage, such as resistance to change, procrastination, hesitancy to ask for help, or tendency to perfectionism. Once brought into conscious awareness, these self-defeating patterns can be examined in light of the core personal values: what is most important to me, and is it important enough to motivate me to overcome patterns in my life that obstruct me from having it?

For some, the support of others is a strength, because they are comfortable interacting with people in their life and willing to ask for help when it is needed. Others may honestly assess support to be a shadow area in their life, e.g., in the form of being too overbearing or too quiet, a codependent need for approval, or a counter dependent insistence of "doing everything myself." The importance of support is an area that the coach must address, identifying whether it is a strength to be emphasized or a shadow to be confronted and mastered. One of the tools available is the MasterMind process for clients to seek like-minded and mutually committed peers to meet with periodically to generate new ideas, reality test older ideas, and share encouragement.

Viktor Frankl[16] asserted three primary sources or types of pathology – somatogenic, psychogenic, and noogenic. The first two are physical and emotional, but the third is existential. This neurotic pathology arises from a perceived emptiness of purpose in life. According to Frankl, the predominant human motivation is the will to meaning; when profound meaning is not perceived, the individual becomes in Frankl's term 'existentially frustrated' or what Pascual-Leone calls 'existentially hopeless'.[17] Frankl[18] used this story to convey the vital importance of purpose, or meaning, in a human being's life:

> Generally, one assumes that a boomerang always returns to the hunter; but actually, I have been told in Australia, a boomerang only comes back to the hunter when it has missed its target. Well, man also only returns to himself, to being concerned with his self, after he has missed his mission, has failed to find a meaning in his life.

Research by Crumbaugh and Maholick[19] validates the perspective that psychopathology tends to increase with perceived lack of purpose in life. Conversely, when a person experiences meaning in his/her life, mental health tends to follow. Clearly, meaning in life and mental health are important components contributing to or detracting from one's motivation. We will revisit the importance of meaning in life as part of the discussion on posttraumatic distress and posttraumatic growth.

## 3.  Containment
A vital function of the coach in the coaching relationship, similar to the function of a therapist in the therapeutic relationship, is "containment"[20]: setting the tone and holding trust in the process. Containing the intensity and tension in interactions does not necessarily mean controlling the direction of those interactions. Indeed, appropriate containment often means allowing, and remaining calm, open, and authentic, in awkward moments of silence, pregnant moments of doubt, even existential angst. "The illusion of being able to direct coaching is one of our defenses against the presence of unpleasant tensions

and doubts."[21] The key question in identifying and navigating through such tensions and doubts is what part of these tensions comes from the client and what originates from the coach? For the coach, containing the interaction means

> being available, asking questions, listening, exploring, and building up a relationship in which critical things can be expressed and critical transitions can be felt. Most of all, it means not avoiding or repressing critical moments when they occur. . . .
> To this end, coaches need a unique combination of warmth and daring, sensitivity and an awareness of boundaries. The best short description of these two almost diametrically opposed characteristics that I have found is in the title of the book by O'Neill (2000): *Coaching With Backbone and Heart;* strength, daring, and containment (*backbone*) to examine the critical moment, and acceptance, readiness, and warmth (*heart*) to welcome and support it.[22]

One important aspect of providing containment is establishing clear healthy boundaries with the client. Coaches must lay down their key conditions in a non-negotiable way from the very beginning so that the clients understand exactly what they are buying into. Those conditions may relate to payment for services, the location of meetings, time commitment for "homework", or many other areas.

## 4. Stages of adult development

Children grow in predictable stages, struggling with a new task until it is mastered, and then incorporating that mastery in engaging the next sequential challenge. The same opportunity for development exists for adults in a lifelong series of stages, although many people essentially stop or dramatically slow down the growth process between age eighteen and their mid-twenties.[23,24,25] There has been a great deal of research on the phenomenon of adult development, and to be effective a coach must be able to bring the concepts into practical application for the client.

The following review of the stages of development in adulthood may be useful to the coach in understanding likely challenges encountered and conclusions being deeply encoded at milestone ages of adult development. This review of developmental periods from early adulthood through the end of life is based on Erikson[26,27], Jung[28], and Levinson[29]. Adulthood is the time to create meaning in life through appropriate decision-making and life-building. One struggles to create authenticity in life, overcoming fear of the unknown and resistance to change. The leading anxieties are unworthiness, the struggle between alienation and connection, and spiritual struggles over the "loss of soul." Ultimately, one must prepare to face one's death anxiety.

Levinson suggests three eras in adult life: early (17 to 45), middle adulthood (40 to 65), and late adulthood (beginning around 60). Adult development evolves through a sequence of age-linked alternating stable and transitional periods, which are characterized by particular developmental tasks. The ages and age ranges suggested by Levinson for the various stages are, of course, only estimates of average attainment of the milestones described. There are always individual variation from these general estimates.

Early adulthood has four distinct developmental periods: a transitional entry period (17-22), a fledgling entry period of building an adult identity (22-28), a transitional period of reappraisal (28-33), and a culminating period of productivity (33-40).

1) The *Early Adult Transition* (from ages 17 to 22) is a developmental bridge between adolescence and early adulthood. This bridge begins a new step in individuation as the budding adult modifies her or his relationships with family, authorities and others, and begins to form a place as an adult in the adult world.

2) The *Entry Period for Early Adulthood* (22-28) is the time for building and maintaining an initial mode of adult living. This is a time for forming and pursuing youthful aspirations, establishing mentor relationships and settling into intimate relationships, and perhaps beginning to raise a family. The individual in this period is buffeted by his/her own passions and ambitions, as well as those imposed by family, community and society. A developmental task is to formulate a Dream, an outcome vision to guide and motivate the pursuit of accomplishment.

3) The *Age 30 Transition* (28-33) is an opportunity to reappraise and modify the entry structure and to create the basis for the coming middle adulthood. This can be a time of career change, going back to school, geographical moves, and upheaval in relationships. The reappraisal may

be disheartening if the individual lacks an organizing Dream.

4)  The *Culmination of Early Adulthood* (33-40) is a time of settling down, of relative stability and satisfaction, of realizing our youthful aspirations or recognizing failure to do so. Which of these dominates this period will determine the quality of the mid-life transition to come: conquest or crisis. This may also be a time of relinquishing, or overthrowing, the mentor relationships in order to step fully into mature adulthood.

Middle adulthood is the timespan from about age 40 to 65, and encompasses the years of recognized achievement and migration to a position of "senior member" within the realms of one's life experiences. "The research indicates, however, that the character of living always changes appreciably between early and middle adulthood."[30] Here again there are four distinct developmental periods: a transitional entry period (40-45), an entry period of establishing a new approach to one's life (45-50), a transitional period of refinement (50-55), and a culminating period to consolidate achievements (55-60).

5)  The *Mid-life Transition* (40-45) is another of the great cross-era shifts, serving both to terminate early adulthood and to initiate middle adulthood. It has become commonplace, a cliché, in our culture for men and women facing this transition to attempt to regain the vitality and passion of their earlier years. This transition is more often than not "one of crisis, where they questioned almost every aspect of their lives, were horrified at what they found, and could not go on as before, although it took several years to form a new path. The transition is important for individuation and personal development to occur and for adapting to the new roles of middle adulthood."[31]

6)  The *Entry Period for Middle Adulthood* (45-50), like its preceding counterpart, provides an initial basis for life in a new era. One has hopefully "become more compassionate, more reflective and judicious, less tyrannized by inner conflicts and external demands, and more genuinely loving of ourselves and others."[32] The alternative is that life has

become increasingly trivial or stagnant.

7) The *Age 50 Transition* (50-55) offers a mid-era opportunity for modifying and perhaps improving the entry life structure. This is perceived as the last chance to make course corrections in order to "get it right." It may be experienced as a crisis by the individual who changed too little in the mid-life transition ten years earlier, and then built an unsatisfactory life on an unacceptable foundation.

8) The *Culmination of Middle Adulthood* (55-60) is the framework in which we conclude this era, the final period of contribution within career and preparation for retirement. Hopefully there is an increased ability to reason with probabilities, an emphasis on context, and a relativity in judgment.

Late adulthood is the timespan from about age 65 on.

9) The *Late Adult Transition* (60-65) is a boundary period between middle and late adulthood, separating and linking the two eras. Individuals must cope with the dawning recognition of moving from "middle age" to "old age."

10) The *Late Adulthood* (60-85) is a time for accommodation to the aging process, for sustaining one's youthful energy and passionate embrace of life in new ways appropriate to late adulthood. And this allows the elder to dispense with the distinction between work and play, to devote him/herself to interests that arise from the very depths of the self. It also means finding a new balance of involvement with society and with the self.

11) The *Late Late Adulthood* (beyond 80) is a time for coming to terms with failing health, the process of dying and preparing for one's impending death. And for deciding to what extent to be engaged in social life and the affairs of humanity, as well as an ultimate involvement with the self. This elder may be able to model for others the nobility of the human spirit.

This discussion of adult development has been in terms of the typical life tasks, responsibilities and challenges that tend to progress along a relatively predictable trajectory as people age.

Research has documented clearly that those at later life stages generally report a greater presence of meaning in their lives, whereas those at earlier life stages report higher levels of searching for meaning. The more meaning in life people report, the greater well-being they experience, at all life stages.[33] Meaning in life will be a recurring theme throughout this book, and is at the heart of successful coaching.

Now we turn our attention to a separate track of development through adulthood: not based on life tasks but rather on advancing maturity, progression toward fulfilling one's potential, i.e., self-actualization.

> Lived experience suggests that some people are "farther along"; some have what we think of as "wisdom," or are "more mature" than others. Still, few people have more than a gut-level sense of this idea of maturity, so it can be hard or impossible to know what to do about an "immature" client. How do you help someone with a narrow perspective? Are all forms of immaturity helped by the same interventions? How can we target our interventions to the particular place of the client? Theories of adult development offer insight into these questions.[34]

Theories of personality (ego) development tend to fall into one of two realms: social–cognitive maturity or social–emotional well-being.[35] The first, rooted in Piaget's[36] theory of cognitive development or Vygotsky's[37] theory of social–cognitive development, deals with *how complexly one thinks* about and understands the self and others. The second, rooted in the theories of Freud[38], Erikson[39], Bowlby[40], and Maslow[41], deals with *how good one feels* about the self in a world of others, with the process of attaining an increasingly more pervasive sense of psychological health and well-being. Social–cognitive maturity is frequently assessed by Loevinger's measure of ego development.[42,43] Social–emotional well-being is often measured by Ryff's[44] Psychological Well-Being assessment.

Research has shown that the two facets of personality development seem to operate independently: people who can think complexly about their lives may or may not be happy; people who are happy may or may not be highly self-reflective. Bauer & McAdams[45] summarize their findings in this regard: "Participants whose life span goals emphasized exploring new perspectives in life, helping others develop, or seeking new challenges seemed especially able to think more complexly about the self and others. Participants who organized their life span goals primarily around attaining happiness, meaningful relationships, or contributing to society (rather than attaining money, status, or approval) were especially likely to have higher levels of well-being." The coach really must know what the client's considered values are in order to truly help him/her maximize them.

Abraham Maslow[46] claimed that people are oriented toward either growth or safety in their everyday lives and that a growth orientation more effectively facilitates psychological health and well-being. What is the connection, then, between ego development and Maslow's hierarchy of needs conceptualization of human motivation, where self-actualization "refers to the desire for self-fulfillment, namely, to the tendency for him to become actualized in what he is potentially."[47]

```
                  /\
                 /  \
                /SELF-\
               /ACTUALIZATION\
              /Pursue Inner Talent\
             /Creativity Fulfillment\
            /------------------------\
           /      SELF-ESTEEM         \
          /  Achievement Mastery       \
         /   Recognition Respect        \
        /------------------------------- \
       /       BELONGING - LOVE           \
      /   Friends Family Spouse Lover      \
     /------------------------------------- \
    /            SAFETY                       \
   /  Security Stability Freedom from Fear     \
  /-------------------------------------------- \
 /            PHYSIOLOGICAL                      \
/      Food Water Shelter Warmth                  \
---------------------------------------------------
```

Individual clients who are oriented to providing for their physical needs, safety, and belonging, who are in need of repairing deficits and dysfunction in their life, are good candidates for psychotherapy. Those who have those basic needs met and are wanting to enhance their self-esteem and achieve mastery in the areas of productivity in life may well benefit from a more positively oriented psychotherapy, or from life coaching. Those who seek self-fulfillment and to manifest their full human potential are asking for facilitation in the process of becoming self-actualized. This is the primary domain of life coaching.

| Reparative psychotherapy | → | Positive psychotherapy | → | Life Coaching |
|---|---|---|---|---|

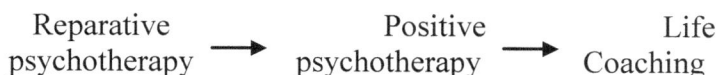

Development beyond the repair of deficits and dysfunction, beyond the maintenance efforts of providing physical needs, safety, and belonging, to becoming *self-actualized* in Maslow's terminology, requires a willingness to take certain risks – emotionally, intellectually, socially. It requires arduous preparation, the courage to be nonconformist, and a willingness to face and overcome one's fears, defenses, and limitations. For example, Maslow[48] spoke about the defenses against growth which keep so many of us from actualizing our full potential despite the impulse in all of us toward self-actualization, or full humanness. One defense Maslow labeled the "fear of one's own greatness" or the "evasion of one's destiny" or the "running away from one's own best talents." Maslow began referring to optimal psychological health and growth as becoming "fully human." And that is the objective of coaching: to encourage and facilitate an individual's development to his/her full human potential.

What does advancing toward self-actualization, or full humanness, look like? In general, ego development is characterized by increasing flexibility; recognition and acceptance of internal contradictions; a broader and more complex understanding of the self, others, and the self in relation to others; internalized self-control and emotional self-regulation. Other qualities associated with self-actualization are a consistent sense of presence, an authenticity, and a lightness or ease of being. Descriptions of people functioning at an optimal level include increasing flexibility, conceptual complexity, and tolerance for ambiguity; recognition and acceptance of internal contradictions; a broader and more complex understanding of the self, others, and the self in relation to others; internalized self-control and emotional self-regulation; transcendence of ego boundaries; transparency; "postambivalence" i.e., total wholehearted and unconflicted love, acceptance, and self-expression.

What Maslow called postambivalence, Jung called an unconditional 'yes' to that which is. In his autobiography *Memories, Dreams, Reflections*, Jung said, "Something else too, came to me from my illness. I might formulate it as an affirmation of things as they are: an unconditional 'yes' to that which is, without subjective protests – acceptance of the conditions of existence as I see them and understand them, acceptance of my own nature, as I happen to be."[49]

Maslow specified eight qualities of a self-actualizing moment[50], qualities that coaches may want to hold up as targets for their clients to aim for:

1. "experiencing fully, vividly, selflessly, with full concentration and total absorption" (p. 44);
2. making the progression choice in a given moment rather than the regression choice, the growth choice instead of the fear choice;
3. letting the self emerge by listening to one's inner voice, what Maslow called the "impulse voices," instead of "Mommy's introjected voice or Daddy's voice or to the voice of the Establishment, of the Elders, of authority, or of tradition" (p. 44);
4. being honest rather than not, taking responsibility for one's beliefs and perspectives;
5. being courageous, not afraid, daring to be different, unpopular, nonconformist;
6. using one's intelligence to go through an arduous and demanding period of preparation in order to realize one's possibilities;
7. setting up the conditions so that peak experiences are more likely by, for example, breaking up an illusion, getting rid of a false notion, learning what one is not good at, learning what one's potentialities are *not*;
8. opening oneself up to one's own psychopathology, identifying defenses and finding the courage to give them up.

All human beings have some aspects of themselves that are less developed than others. One's best intentions and strongest character traits can be held ransom in arrested development by one's unresolved shadow aspects, in spite of the individual's general accelerated stage of development. Due to unconscious self-sabotage, many people actually operate in their life at a lower level of success than they are capable of. There are known practices which "unfreeze" arrested development, allowing the individual to move beyond such limitations, and we will review a number of them in this book. One of the most fundamental is any systematic practice for experiencing transcendence.[51] Through transcendent experience, the self-concept "becomes increasingly differentiated, fragmented, elusive and ultimately transparent."[52] The highly developed ego, through its transparency to itself, is able to achieve a "therapeutic split,"[53] becoming both subject and object, observer and observed, a witness to the dynamic flow of psychic events. This "witness consciousness" and the self-transcendence upon which it is based are also foundational ingredients of higher stages of human development.

This process of "unfreezing" aspects of oneself that are held hostage to arrested development, of course, applies on different levels to each layer of intervention: reparative psychotherapy, positive psychotherapy, and life coaching.

Late in his life, Maslow added an ultimate level of development beyond self-actualization, which he called *self-transcendence*; he variously conceptualized it as seeking a benefit beyond the purely personal; seeking communion with the transcendent, perhaps through mystical or transpersonal experiences; identifying with something greater than the purely individual self, often engaging in service to others. "The earlier model positions the highest form of motivational development at the level of the well-adjusted, differentiated, and fulfilled individual self or ego. The later model places the highest form of human development at a transpersonal level, where the self/ego and its needs are transcended."[54]

Maslow[55] eventually distinguished *transcending self-actualizing* individuals, described as exhibiting "unitive perception," or the "fusion of the eternal with the temporal, the sacred with the profane"[56] from what he called *nontranscending self-actualizers.*[57] He described such people as "more essentially practical, realistic, mundane, capable, and secular people, living more in the here and now world . . . 'doers' rather than meditators or contemplators, effective and pragmatic rather than aesthetic, reality-testing and cognitive rather than emotional and experiencing."[58] Due to this observation, in his unpublished critique of self-actualization theory[59], Maslow thought that "self-actualization is not enough"[60] for a full picture of the optimally functioning human being. In an essay titled *Theory Z*, Maslow wrote[61]

> I have recently found it more and more useful to differentiate between two kinds (or better, degrees) of self-actualizing people, those who were clearly healthy, but with little or no experiences of transcendence, and those in whom transcendent experiencing was important and even central. As examples of the former kind of health, I may cite Mrs. Eleanor Roosevelt, and, probably, Truman and Eisenhower. As examples of the latter, I can use Aldous Huxley, and probably Schweitzer, Buber, and Einstein.
>
> . . . I am more likely to find cognizing of transcendence not only in self-actualizing but also in highly creative or talented people, in highly intelligent people, in very strong characters, in powerful and responsible leaders and managers, in exceptionally good (virtuous) people and in "heroic" people who have overcome adversity and who have been strengthened by it rather than weakened.

Observable mental health may or may not correlate directly with advanced levels of ego development. An individual operating at the transcending self-actualized level may, in fact, display *more* pathological or dysfunctional symptoms than one who is operating at the non-transcending self-actualizing level. Maslow referred to *value pathologies*, what he also called *metapathologies*, which are the spiritual-existential ailments of cynicism, apathy, boredom, loss of zest, despair, hopelessness, a sense of powerlessness, and nihilism.[62] The coach's legitimate realm of intervention certainly includes addressing such self-sabotaging patterns, just as it does working with similar patterns in the lives of individuals operating at any level of development.

Maslow spoke further about the defense he called 'fear of one's own greatness'. "We fear our highest possibilities (as well as our lowest ones). We are generally afraid to become that which we can glimpse in our most perfect moments, under the most perfect conditions."[63] He also suggests that this fear serves a positive purpose: it is a defense against grandiosity, arrogance, sinful pride, hubris. To invent or create, to step into one's own greatness, one must have the "arrogance of creativeness." But if one has *only* the arrogance without an offsetting humility, then the "self-crippling" becomes destructive. Maslow uses Aldous Huxley as an example of someone who accepted his talents and used them to the full, while looking out at the world with wide eyes, with unabashed innocence, awe and fascination, "which is a kind of admission of smallness, a form of humility."[64] This sense of humility is another foundational ingredient of higher stages of human development; it activates self-transcendence, or transcending the ego.

Beyond the ordinary adult ego structure lies a potential and optional advanced ego, which we might call the *transcendental ego* or *ultraself*.[65] Maslow[66] compiled a set of qualities that distinguish transcending self-actualizers from nontranscending self-actualizers, and that may serve as markers for the presence of one's ultraself. We present here a summary of his characteristics of transcending self-actualizers, or transcenders. These qualities reflect a different set of values along the continuum of social–cognitive maturity or social–emotional well-being. The coach of course needs to ascertain clearly the client's own core values, being careful not to make assumptions but to listen actively and question assertively. The distinction between these two types of self-actualizers should not be seen as a mandate to move a client from nontranscending to transcending status. Rather, it may be helpful in the ongoing process of assessing core values and core strengths.

1. For the transcenders, peak experiences and plateau experiences become *the* most important things in their lives, the most precious aspect of life.
2. They speak naturally and unconsciously the language of Being (B-language), the language of poets, of mystics, of seers, of profoundly religious men, of men who live under the aspect of eternity, the language of parable and paradox.
3. They perceive unitively the sacred within the secular, i.e., the sacredness in all things *at the same time* that they also see them at the practical, everyday level. This ability is in *addition* to—not mutually exclusive with—good reality testing.
4. They are much more consciously and deliberately metamotivated by the values of perfection, truth, beauty, goodness, unity, dichotomy-transcendence.
5. They seem somehow to recognize each other, and to come to almost instant intimacy and mutual understanding even upon first meeting.

6. They are *more* responsive to beauty, or rather they tend to beautify all things.
7. They are *more* holistic about the world than are the "healthy" or practical self-actualizers (who are also holistic in this same sense). Mankind is one, and such limiting concepts as the "national interest" or "the religion of my fathers" or "different grades of people or of IQ" either cease to exist or are easily transcended.
8. Overlapping this statement of holistic perceiving is a strengthening of the self-actualizer's natural tendency to synergy—intrapsychic, interpersonal, intracultural.
9. They transcend the ego (the Self, the identity) more often and more easily.
10. Not only are such people lovable, but they are also more awe-inspiring, more "unearthly, more easily revered." They more often produced in Maslow the thought, "This is a great man."
11. Transcenders are far more apt to be innovators, discovers of the new, of what actually *could* be, what exists *in potential*.
12. They can be more ecstatic, more rapturous than the happy and healthy ones, yet maybe more prone to a kind of cosmic-sadness over the stupidity of people, their self-defeat, their blindness, their cruelty to each other, their shortsightedness.
13. Transcenders can more easily live in both the D- and B-realms (Deficit and Being realms) simultaneously than can the merely healthy self-actualizers because they can sacralize everybody so much more easily. The way of phrasing this paradox that Maslow found useful is this: The factually "superior" transcending self-actualizer acts always to the factually "inferior" person as to a brother, a member of the family who must be loved and cared for no matter what he does because he is after all a member of the family.
14. Peak-experiencers and transcenders in particular, as well as self-actualizers in general, find mystery is *attractive* and challenging rather than frightening. In contrast, most people pursue knowledge to lessen mystery and thereby reduce anxiety. The self-actualizer is apt to be bored by

what is well known, however useful this knowledge may be, and encountering new knowledge to be awed before the tremendousness of the universe. At the highest levels of development of humanness, knowledge leads to a sense of mystery, awe, humility, ultimate ignorance, and reverence.

15. Transcenders are less afraid of "nuts" and "kooks" than are other self-actualizers, and are also more able to screen out the apparent nuts and kooks who are *not* creative contributors.

16. Transcenders tend to be more "reconciled with evil" in the sense of understanding its occasional inevitability and necessity in the larger holistic sense. Since this implies a better understanding of apparent evil, it generates *both* a greater compassion with it *and* a less ambivalent and more decisive, more unyielding fight against it.

17. Transcenders are more apt to regard themselves as *carriers* of talent, *instruments* of the transpersonal, temporary custodians so to speak of a greater intelligence or skill or leadership or efficiency. This means a certain particular kind of objectivity or detachment toward themselves that to nontranscenders might sound like arrogance, grandiosity, or even paranoia. Transcendence brings with it a "transpersonal" loss of ego.

18. Transcenders are more apt to be profoundly "religious" or "spiritual" in either the theistic or nontheistic sense, excluding their historical, conventional, superstitious, institutional meanings.

19. Transcenders find it easier to transcend the ego, the self, the identity, i.e., to go beyond self-actualization. Nontranscending self-actualizers are primarily strong identities, people who know who they are, where they are going, what they want, what they are good for, using themselves well and authentically and in accordance with their own true nature. Transcenders are certainly this; but they are also more than this.

20. Transcenders, because of their easier perception of the B-realm, have more end experiences than their more

practical brothers do, more of the fascinations that we see in children who get hypnotized by the colors in a puddle, or by raindrops dripping down a windowpane, or by the smoothness of skin, or the movements of a caterpillar.

21. Transcenders are somewhat more Taoistic; the merely healthy somewhat more pragmatic. B-cognition makes everything look more miraculous, more perfect, just as it *should* be. It therefore breeds less impulse to *do* anything to the object that is fine just as it is, less needing improvement, or intruding upon.

22. "Postambivalence" tends to be more characteristic of all self-actualizers and perhaps a little more so in transcenders. This concept from Freudian theory means total wholehearted and unconflicted love, acceptance, expressiveness, rather than the more usual mixture of love and hate that passes for "love" or friendship or authority.

23. With increasing maturity of character, higher forms of reward and metareward other than money and acknowledgment steadily *increase* in importance, while money is recognized as a symbol for status, success, and self-esteem with which to win love, admiration, and respect.

Higher levels of ego development have been related to changes over time in levels of responsibility, tolerance, and achievement via independence[67] as well as to ego resiliency and interpersonal integrity.[68]

There is a distinct correlation between the types of psychopathology and level of ego development.[69] Use of immature defenses, such as projection, repression, and "acting out" are negatively related to ego level, whereas more mature defense mechanisms, such as rationalization and reversal, are positively related to ego development. Ego-resiliency, that is, the capacity to manage anxiety and to rebound from frustrating experiences, is also positively related to ego development.[70]

Let's address here an important aspect of any discussion of progression through stages of development. People progress in fits and spurts; there are periods of quantum steps followed by periods of consolidation. Advancing to a next stage is a process, not like crossing a line at one point in time. And the process can be somewhat quantified.

> Many people have a center of gravity with about 25% of their scores at the level below. This reflects where they are consolidating into the center of gravity. Additionally, they generally have about 25% of their answers at the level above their center of gravity. Answers above their center of gravity reflect their growing edge. . . . Leading edge represents the areas where one is developing toward a later developmental level while lagging edge represents the areas one is consolidating from earlier developmental levels.[71]

This discussion of adult development through stages is important for a life coach to use as an overall paradigm in terms of assisting clients to assess current weaknesses as areas in consolidation, and current challenges as leading edges of growth. It is important in assisting clients to identify goals and in setting priorities. It is important in clarifying clients' level and arena of motivation.

## 5.   The human energy system and energy management

One very practical aspect of a client's life that needs attention from the coach is the physiological energy configuration and how the client is using (or abusing) it. One important example is the sympathetic and parasympathetic branches of the nervous system. The sympathetic branch activates to respond to an event proactively, "taking the bull by the horns" or running away from the bull, but in either case acting assertively. The parasympathetic response is to avoid, to take the time to digest all relevant data, to "sleep on it", or to become paralyzed with indecision or fear of acting. In life coaching, one needs to be prepared to question the client's energetic tendencies, to challenge the responses that may be self-sabotaging and to encourage those that are healthy and productive.

Trauma and shock affect a person's life choices, and it is the purview of psychotherapy to discover and heal any residual pathology from traumatic experiences. But the coach also must be aware of the life patterns that developed out of trauma, because they are foundational to current day shadows that cripple core strengths and interfere with attaining core values. Here we might look to the field of traumatic resiliency, or posttraumatic growth, to enumerate the coach's approach to dealing with residual trauma. We are assuming that the coaching client has succeeded in reparative psychotherapy, and is ready to engage the challenges of optimal development, of finding meaning in adversity, and advancing toward transcending self-actualization. In other words, the client has journeyed along the previously identified continuum sufficiently to make the most of his/her coaching opportunity.

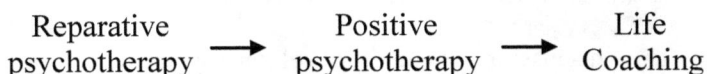

Reparative psychotherapy ➤ Positive psychotherapy ➤ Life Coaching

Energy of a particular nature is contagious – shared automatically, unintentionally, uncontrollably – and it is important for the coach to be alert to the contagious influence of the client's energy, and to consciously self-regulate his/her own energy. For example, if the client is experiencing an activated sympathetic response, such as fear, anxiety, or panic, obviously the coach needs to maintain a calming, reflective energy. Likewise, if the client has descended into a parasympathetic response such as helplessness, defeat, or suddenly "feeling tired", the coach must avoid the contagion of that energy and maintain an alert, optimistic stance. To do so requires conscious self-monitoring and the ability to self-regulate. And this skill is important to teach to the client, which occurs through modeling it as well as direct suggestion.

This energy contagion is related to, but separate from, emotional contagion[72], i.e., "the tendency to automatically mimic and synchronize facial expressions, vocalizations, postures, and movements with those of another person and, consequently, to converge emotionally." Examples would be when smiles elicit smiles, or when a fist raised in anger causes a timid person to shrink back in fear. And the moods of the leader in a relationship, the boss or supervisor or coach, is more contagious than those of others.[73] The coach can utilize this tendency, of course, by modeling a positive emotion for a client who is experiencing annoyance (anger), jealousy, or worry (fear).

An awareness of the major energy vortexes in the body, known as chakra energy centers, is helpful in assessing the client's values and strengths, from moment to moment as well as on a longitudinal basis. The chakra energy centers can be seen as a somatic expression of Maslow's Hierarchy of Needs as described earlier. The root chakra, at the base of the spine, is consumed with physiological and existential survival. The second or sacral chakra, three inches below the navel, is related primarily to safety, security, and passionate experience in life. The third chakra, located at the solar plexus, is concerned with personal power, integrity, and freedom from fear. The fourth chakra, located at the heart, is all about love, belonging, and compassion. The fifth chakra, located at the throat, regulates one's self-esteem, expression of essence in the world, and one's sense of mastery. The sixth chakra, known as the third-eye, is located in the center of the head and is the locus for personal identity and vision of one's potential future self. The seventh chakra, located at the crown or fontanel of the head, is activated with self-transcendence and inspiration from above.

As people progress to higher levels of self development, they tend to process their experience more along the following lines: (1) cognitively, the more integrated the brain, the more complexly it is capable of incorporating more diverse sources of input; (2) affectively, one becomes less reactive and less defensive, more open and more spontaneous; and (3) behaviorally, people become more likely to take action based on intentional conscious choice in light of clear life purpose.

Integration includes *top-down* or *high road* (cognitive) and *bottom-up* or *low road* (affect/body) *processing*. Safran and Greenberg[74] have described the difference between these two ways in which we operate. Top-down change usually involves exploring and challenging tacit rules and beliefs that guide the processing of emotional experience, whereas bottom-up processing begins with the experiential and leads eventually to change at the verbal-representational and conceptual level. Individuals at lower levels of ego development seem to operate primarily by means of bottom-up information processing, whereas at higher stages people are more capable of blending bottom-up with top-down processing. Thus, emotion which is usually processed unconsciously in the amygdala to produce a reaction of fight/ flight/ or freeze, can take the high road of deliberation and conscious choice in the frontal cortex. In this way, for example, reactive conditioned anger can be refined into "mindfully-held anger" in which anger is consciously contained and observed instead of being expressed, or into "heart-anger" in which anger is mindfully and compassionately expressed.[75] An individual who is sufficiently developed can override the immediate, unconscious response and initiate a more thoughtful and intentional alternative. However, this is a far cry from repression, suppression, denial, or spiritual bypass.

> The amygdala, as well as being activated automatically, receives input from the cortex, allowing for conscious processing to affect emotionality . . . This suggests the operation of a second level of emotional processing, involving complex perceptions and concepts received from the cortex, but this occurs only after a more immediate intuitive appraisal by the emotional brain from the initial input. LeDoux (1996) thus has suggested that there are two different paths for producing emotion: What he terms the *low* road, when the amygdala senses danger and broadcasts an emergency distress signal to brain and body, and the slower *high* road, in which the same information is carried through the thalamus to the neocortex. Because the shorter amygdaloid pathway transmits signals more than twice as fast as the neocortex route, the thinking brain often cannot intervene in time to stop emotional responses.[76]

Bill Torbert[77] makes the same comparison regarding people's attention, namely that it normally runs *downstream*. Thoughts are stimulated by something in the environment, either intentionally or randomly. As an individual becomes more conscious, more intentional, more highly developed, the processing attends more to self-observation: the *upstream* flow of attention flows back from questioning what is my experience, what is my impact on the world, what is my overall strategy, and ultimately how am I attending to my experience in the first place.

Clearly, gaining conscious choice over reactivity, by activating the neocortex before the amygdala can generate an unconscious emotional response, requires mindful self-awareness. The mindful option is also promoted through more ordered and coherent heart rhythms, the somatic manifestation of mindfulness (the clear and calm experience of reality without attachment or judgment), stimulated through conscious breathing techniques. Coherent heart rhythms, measured as heart-rate variability (HRV), reduce nervous system chaos, facilitate cortical function, increase access to clear and effective thinking, problem-solving discernment, memory recall, connection with core values, heartbrain synchronization, emotional stability, and spiritual connectedness.[78,79]

The integration of which we speak occurs on other levels than emotional processing, attentional processing, and heart rhythm coherence. For example, human beings are highly associational, and so a recent experience may trigger something that occurred in the past. Integrating those patterns of habitual response through self-awareness and increasing self-regulation brings more opportunities to make conscious choices about how to react. Human beings are highly interrelated, and self development includes gaining awareness of the amazing system of mirror neurons that allows us to pick up and feel the feelings and intentions of others, intuitively and unconsciously. Accessing deep primary process elements of the right hemisphere and linking them to the verbal meaning-making capacity of the left, creates new neural connections that literally foster integrative states in the nervous system and the heart.[80,81]

## 6.   Understanding stress, overwhelm and burn-out

Life coaching requires that we assess the degree of stress in the client's life, and determine whether it has escalated to the level of overwhelm or even to burn-out. Highly productive people tend to be ambitious, and that usually involves a certain amount of stress. If the individual does not provide enough self-nurturance, the stress accumulates and can become overwhelming. The entrepreneurial type often tends to deal with overwhelm by trying harder, working more, and increasing the sense of pressure to produce. Burn-out is not far off.

Resilience and serenity consist of appropriate use of both *positive assertive* and *positive yielding* control. The Serenity Prayer summarizes this resilience: "God, grant me the courage to change what I can, the serenity to accept what I cannot change, and the wisdom to know the difference." Shapiro[82] identifies four distinct modes or characteristic ways of gaining a sense of control: *positive assertive*, exercising competent decision-making authority by altering oneself or the environment as needed; p*ositive yielding*, letting go of active control efforts and accepting the situation without helplessness; n*egative assertive*, uncontained aggressive self-sufficiency resulting in constriction in relationships and inability to express or let go within oneself; n*egative yielding*, passivity resulting in denial of self and helplessness. Research findings by Astin and associates[83] suggest that balanced use of active and yielding control efforts may lead to optimal psychosocial adjustment and quality of life even in the face of life-threatening illnesses, including cancer.

Recall the paradoxical stance of the *transcender* described by Maslow as postambivalence and by Jung as an unconditional 'yes' to that which is. A client whose developmental center of gravity is not at the transcending level may not yet be ready to The effective life coach will assist clients to discern and implement the optimal balance of active and yielding control to suit their current level of development – the client's, not the coach's!

Two executive coaches, Eric Nelson and Robert Hogan, recognize that, "Personality characteristics predict leadership effectiveness and, by extension, organizational outcomes."[84] And those personality characteristics can degrade executive effectiveness – what they call the 'dark side' of personality, the dysfunctional interpersonal and self-regulatory patterns that interfere with one's ability to capitalize on their strengths and achieve excellence and mastery. These flawed behavior patterns reflect the influence of underlying mental models that we call early conclusions and decisions. We encode our perceptions of social interaction through the unconscious screen of these beliefs. An example is an individual who was frequently criticized early in life, who may develop the deep-seated belief that he is likely to be criticized in current interpersonal encounters, and even to interpret innocuous feedback as critical. Willing to do almost anything to minimize the risk of being criticized by others, or anything he might construe as criticism, he may become overly perfectionistic or accommodating.

An effective coach will be alert to such self-defeating unconscious beliefs, and will find ways of bringing the client's awareness to them so that they can be transformed into more productive perspectives. We will discuss specific methods of accomplishing this later in the "Heart-Centered Approach to Coaching" section.

## 7.  Quieting the mind
Quieting the mind is an important antidote to excess stress and overwhelm, and a coach should be a resource to clients regarding ways of doing so. Any quiet reflection time that

accesses the brain's default mode network is helpful for accessing inspiration, vision, and creativity. Guided imagery techniques can provide the structure that some people need to accomplish the same thing. Meditation techniques quiet the mind and position one to listen for inner guidance. Mindfulness is an approach to staying present in one's daily life that prepares one to be and stay focused and yet observant with a wide angle lens.

It is appropriate for a coach to inquire about clients' spirituality as a resource in their life, yet while some coaches may feel qualified to offer "Spiritual Direction", it is a separate function and should not be incorporated as an integral aspect of the coaching they offer unless it was clearly accepted by the client in the initial coaching agreement.

There is a path to mindfulness, or rather many paths, and they seem to be very consistently prescribed by wisdom traditions across cultures and history. The three basic elements needed for transformational work are summarized by Sanchez and Vieira[85]:

- presence (awareness, mindfulness)
- the practice of self-observation, gained from self-knowledge
- understanding what one's experiences mean (an accurate interpretation provided by a larger context such as a community, a teacher, or a spiritual system).

Mindfulness is a term that has come into general use, often without precise definition. The concept has historical roots in several related mental processes, as discussed by Martin[86,87]: *deautomatization* and the *observing self*[88], *decentering*[89], *mindfulness as a creative cognitive process*[90], *detachment*[91], and *mental freedom*[92]. Each of these interrelated and overlapping concepts contribute to a fuller understanding of mindfulness, which Martin defines as "a state of psychological freedom that occurs when attention remains quiet and limber, without attachment to any particular point of view."

Hick[93] utilizes the following working definition of mindfulness, collated from definitions by Kabat-Zinn[94], Shapiro[95], and Segal[96]: "a nonelaborative, nonjudgmental, present-centered awareness in which each thought, feeling or sensation that arises in the attentional field is acknowledged and

accepted as it is." There are three primary components to
mindfulness: paying attention, purposefully or with intention,
and with an attitude of openness and nonjudgmentalness.
Attention involves observing, noticing, bringing awareness in the
present moment, with beginner's mind. Intention involves a
personal commitment to participate in one's present-moment
experience with the specific purpose of heightened receptivity to
the internal and external environment. Openness to experience
may be operationalized as non-defensiveness, willingness to
share experiences, openness to the unknown and unknowable, to
emotions, ideas and spirituality, and to seeming
incompatibilities.

Cassandra Vieten and her co-authors[97] identify predictors,
mediators, outcomes, and developmental milestones that appear
to be common to the process of spiritual transformation. They
define transformation as a "profound shift in our human
experience of consciousness that results in long-lasting shifts in
worldview or ways of being and changes in the general pattern
of the way one experiences and relates to oneself, others, and the
world. Spiritual transformation is transformation that occurs
through spiritual experience or practice." Spiritual
transformation has also been defined as a "radical reorganization
of one's identity, meaning, and purpose in life".[98]

Vieten et al. speak of transformation as a turning of attention
and a redirecting of intention that shifts the entire landscape and
one's trajectory through it. Common words used by research
subjects to describe this shift in perspective are "opening," "a
larger, wider, more inclusive and expanded depth perception," "a
shift in worldview, assumptions, values, and beliefs," "a
perception of vastness and being in touch with a larger
consciousness," and "an expanded awareness."

Vieten's respondents reported an expanded worldview and
an alteration of one's sense of self, often described as radical
widening and deepening of one's personal identity. Many
respondents described spiritual experiences of awakening to a
witnessing self fundamentally distinct from particular thoughts,
impulses, feelings, or sensations, accompanied by a feeling of
being more real, more genuine, more authentically themselves. A
part of many spiritual experiences involved less sense of a
personal identity and a greater sense of connection to others,

leading to less reactivity and judgmentalness, and a greater sense of compassion for one's own and others' failings.

Other words used to describe this shift in sense of self from a self-centered perspective to a more communal sense of self: "a deep connection with all of life," "feeling aligned with a greater force," "a deepening into the self," "less feeling of fragmentation and isolation," "a feeling of not being separate, of being interconnected," "a realization that 'I am part of a consciousness that is so much bigger'."

The most common indicator across traditions of a "transformed" person was a consistent sense of presence, an authenticity, and a lightness or ease of being, across situations. Other words commonly used to describe a transformed person were: childlike, simple, transparent, loving, wise, compassionate, patient, tolerant, forgiving, collaborative, mindful, solid, real, whole and possessing the qualities of equanimity, integrity, peace of mind, generosity and a deep acceptance of self and others as they are. Others characterized this state of being by what was *not* present – i.e., not ego-driven, ostentatious, achievement-oriented, narcissistic, not hiding anything, and not necessarily perfect or having everything worked out, but bearing difficulties and failings with grace and humor.

One enduring outcome commonly reported was the presence of an observing or witnessing self, described as a heightened awareness, detachment, or mindfulness, of one's experience, regardless of the content. Another commonly reported outcome that remained present in times of difficulty was an increased ability to stay open, to allow, to not attempt to avoid, contract, resist or harden in response to painful experience. An increased capacity for acceptance and compassion toward self and others in times of conflict was also a theme. An overarching theme was less reactivity to painful experience and a greater self-efficacy for coping.

Peak experiences such as moments of insight or epiphany are often followed by plateaus. Such insights can fade quickly without the presence of a "scaffolding" for the learning process to assist with making meaning of the unfamiliar experience, such as: (1) having a language and cultural context for the experience, bringing it from unconsciousness to conscious awareness; (2) having supportive like-minded community, including contact with more experienced practitioners (also necessary for ego development); (3) encountering or intentionally placing daily reminders of the experience in one's environment, which in NLP terms are called *anchors*; (4) continuing to access similar teachings; or (5) expressing the insight through art, writing or other action (using the sensual alpha brain wave state as a bridge from deep subliminal theta experience to everyday mind beta experience). The process is inhibited by lack of quiet solitude, not enough time in nature, staying too busy, and too quickly returning to contexts apathetic or inimical to transformation.

## 8.  Critical moments

In coaching there is the ever-present feeling that something key may happen at any time, a tangible turning point, something that will have important consequences. The tension arises around the fact that we don't know what it may be, which consequences may follow (positive or negative?), or when such a special moment may appear. These decisive moments are referred to in the literature as *turning points*[99], *now-moments*[100], or *critical moments*.[101,102]

Critical moments are defined as exciting, tense, or significant moments from the time spent in the coaching conversation experienced by a coach and one of his clients.[103] Such moments generate and carry tension and anxiety, and at the same time a heightened sense of poignancy. Effective coaching requires one to ask how might one make constructive use of such tensions rather than avoiding or rushing past the rich opportunity they present?

> In my view, *external* tensions (stemming from the coachee's material and presentation) obstruct the coach only if they give rise to *internal* tensions, that is, if they influence the coach's ability to put things into perspective, his detachment and his patience. It is therefore vitally important for the coach to learn how to handle his own internal tensions—to allow those internal tensions to exist, to note their presence but at the same time to reserve some attention for perceptions, hunches, making connections and other coaching interventions. (de Haan, 2008b, p. 128).

A "moment" in conversation is defined to last between 2 and 8 seconds.[104] So in a coaching interaction of 60 or 90 minutes, there are many hundreds of moments. An interesting finding in the research is that coach and client virtually always identify one or more critical moments that occur in every coaching session, and in almost half of the descriptions, the coach and the client refer to the same moments as being critical in a given coaching session.

Examples of critical moments are a moment of learning a new insight, a moment of learning a new connection or perspective, a positive or negative change in the coach-coachee relationship, or a sense of significance in a moment of self-doubt. It may be a sudden breakthrough experience, a moment of shared humor, a 'what next?' moment, or an experience of deep personal doubt. Doubts and critical moments form a starting point for significant learning experiences ("breakthroughs"). This is true to the extent that the coach is capable of containing the tension and doubt, and using it constructively. In fact, "the quality of an experienced coach's work is determined primarily by their ability to tolerate tension and deliberately inquire into tensions within coaching relationships."[105]

"The main question in the coaching of critical situations is 'how do I keep this tension in the room?' Or in other words, 'how do I keep my coachee in doubt?' or 'how can I extend the time to examine this doubt as a doubt and continue to learn from it?' "[106]

Some of the coaching techniques that lead coachees to critical moments and to breakthroughs are
1. Questioning unexamined assumptions;
2. Summarizing, paraphrasing, reviewing and mirroring the coachee's statements to bring a new perspective;
3. Reflecting back and giving honest and direct feedback;
4. Offering self revelations and personal examples;
5. Introducing a "right-brain" approach such as a guided imagery to explore untapped potentials, walking a timeline to explore difficult options; using each hand to represent opposing drives and to explore potential integration; and
6. Confronting the coaching relationship in the moment – transference/ countertransference – and making it explicit.

## 9. Strengths

We have emphasized the vital importance of focusing on a client's strengths and passions, as well as values. It is those strengths that provide the raw materials, and passions that provide the engine of motivation to achieve. Every coaching interaction should include reference to the client's strengths. That can be assessed informally through discussion, or in a structured way through an assessment tool such as the Values in Action Inventory of Strengths (assessment available for free at www.viastrengths.org from The Mayerson Foundation, creators of the VIA Institute). The instrument is a powerful pathway to greater self-awareness of strengths. It is one of the coach's most important tasks to help clients discover their greatest strengths, and then to remind them of those strengths frequently.

Strengths assessment instruments like the VIA Inventory of Strengths identify *how* people do things. As a coach working to define strengths, we might have individuals first write down "what" they do well; their strong tasks and abilities. Then they might differentiate *what* from *how* strengths, since the *how* strengths can be applied to multiple tasks. Identifying the difference helps clients prioritize their tasks with both *what* they do well and *how* they do them well.[107] Encourage clients to redesign their day by placing their *what* strengths at optimal times during the day as energizers, or rewards for doing difficult tasks, then identify where their *how* strengths can make the day or tasks more efficient and more enjoyable.

S*elf-concept* in the psychological literature is described as the individual's overall view of the self.[108,109] It includes these three components:

1. an *ideal self* – the kind of person they would like to be,
2. a *self-image* – the kind of person they think they are now, and
3. *self-esteem* –how good they feel about themselves based on their self-evaluation.

If one could measure the discrepancy between the ideal self and actual self (self-image), it would indicate the person's level of self-esteem. William James defined self-esteem as "the ratio of our actualities to our supposed potentialities."[110]

Faced with a clear discrepancy, there are several possible courses of action that will resolve it in a way that increases self-esteem. One is to re-affirm the rightness of the ideal, and to set out to improve one's capabilities, build on strengths, become more effective, and grow closer to that ideal self. In other words, after honest self-appraisal the individual finds renewed motivation to improve and excel.

Another is to re-assess the appropriateness of the ideal in the first place. It may be unrealistic, based on perfectionist fantasy, and modifying it may well lead to greater productivity, satisfaction and self-esteem. Also, often that ideal was instilled in us by others, perhaps parents who wanted their child to be a star football player, a white swan ballerina, or an egghead intellectual. Discovering that one's ideal self is not really a reflection of one's own aspirations can lead to a search for our *true self*, based on our own values and meaning in life. Needless to say, striving to be what one is not can never result in the highest expression of an individual's essential self.

An effective coach will work with a client to understand the internal dynamics of self-esteem; that is, the relationship between self-image and ideal self. One way to do that is to look at one's historical approach to resolving any discrepancies. Individuals may have ideals in line with their self-image in one area of their life and an ideal wildly out of alignment in another; for example, living a fulfilling life professionally, at work, but feel they are falling far short of their potential in personal relationships, at home.[111]

Martin Seligman has worked out a blueprint for happiness that people can use to set them on the path to a fulfilling and satisfying life. He believes there are three routes to happiness, which he calls the "pleasant life", the "good life" and the "meaningful life." A mix of all three is ideal.

The pleasant life sees superficial pleasures as the key to happiness. To be seriously happy, we have to set our sights on a good life and a meaningful life. To do this we need to identify our signature strengths and use them in our working and social lives to help us achieve "a good life", while using them to help others will put us on course for achieving a "meaningful life." Listed here are the six virtues, or core values, and the signature strengths that support each.[112,113]

**Wisdom** - the ability to take stock of life in large terms, in ways that make sense to oneself and others
- **Curiosity in the world** - an ongoing, intrinsic interest in both their inner experience and the world around them. Curious people tend to be attracted to new people, new things, and new experiences, and they are rarely bored.
- **Love of learning** - motivated to acquire new skills or knowledge or to build on existing skills or knowledge. They feel good when they are learning new things, even though they may occasionally become frustrated when the material is challenging.
- **Judgment, critical thinking and open-mindedness** - the willingness to search actively for evidence against one's favored beliefs, plans, or goals, and to weigh such evidence fairly when it is available
- **Ingenuity, originality**, practical intelligence, street smarts
- **Social intelligence**, personal intelligence, emotional intelligence
- **Perspective** - Providing wise counsel to others

**Courage**
- **Valor and bravery** - Acting on convictions without shrinking from threat or difficulty.
- **Perseverance**, industry and diligence - voluntary continuation of a goal-directed action in spite of obstacles, difficulties, or discouragement
- **Integrity**, Genuineness, honesty - A regular pattern of behavior that is consistent with espoused values (i.e., "practicing what you preach").

**Humanity and Love**
- **Kindness and Generosity** - generosity, nurturance, care, compassion, and altruistic love
- **Loving** and allowing oneself to be loved
- **Justice** - Civic strengths that underlie healthy community life.
- **Fairness and equity** - Giving everyone a fair chance, treating people the same according to a sense of justice.
- **Leadership** - Organizing group activities and seeing that they happen.

**Temperance**
- **Self control** - Being disciplined, controlling appetites and emotions.
- **Prudence**, discretion, caution - *Prudence is a cognitive orientation to the personal future, a form of practical reasoning and self-management that helps to achieve the individual's long-term goals effectively. Prudent individuals show a farsighted and deliberate concern for the consequences of their actions and decisions, successfully resisting impulses and other choices that satisfy shorter term goals at the expense of longer term ones, having a flexible and moderate approach to life, and striving for balance among their goals and ends.*
- **Humility and modesty** - Letting accomplishments speak for themselves, not seeking limelight.

**Transcendence**
- **Appreciation of beauty and excellence** - ability to find, recognize, and take pleasure in the existence of goodness in the physical and social worlds.
- **Gratitude** - Being thankful for the good things that happen.
- **Hope, optimism and future-mindedness** - Expecting the best and believing one can work to achieve it.
- **Spirituality**, sense of purpose, faith, religiousness - a concept of an ultimate, transcendent, sacred, and divine force that guides an individual's daily life experience
- **Forgiveness and mercy** - a series of changes that occur within an individual who has been offended or hurt in some way by another person. When individuals forgive, their thoughts and actions toward the transgressor become more positive (e.g., more peaceful or compassionate) and less negative (e.g., less wrathful or avoidant).
- **Playfulness and humor** - Seeing the light side, bringing smiles and laughter.
- **Zest, passion and enthusiasm** - Approaching life with excitement and energy; not doing things halfway or halfheartedly; living life as an adventure; feeling alive and activated

According to Seligman[114], Positive Psychology has three pillars. The first is the study of positive emotion. The second is the study of positive traits, foremost among them the virtues, but also "abilities" such as intelligence and athleticism. Third is the study of positive institutions that support the virtues, such as democracy, strong families, and free inquiry.

Seligman's work on optimism is one platform upon which Positive Psychology is based. When pessimists suffer a loss or defeat in life, they attribute it to causes that are long-lasting or permanent, pervasively affecting everything, and that are uncontrollable and yet their own fault. By contrast, optimists regard defeat and loss as temporary, limited to the present case, and as being changeable, i.e., the result of circumstances, bad luck, or the actions of other people.

Another of the platforms for Positive Psychology comes from the research and writing of Mihaly Csikszentmihalyi[115] and his concept of 'flow'. When do you find yourself doing exactly what you want to be doing, and never wanting it to end? When we are in flow we concentrate; there are clear goals; we get immediate feedback; we have deep, effortless involvement; there is a sense of control; our sense of self vanishes; time stops.

Three things reliably predict a heightened sense of gratification and fulfillment for adults: 1) being in a romantic relationship that we consider stable; 2) being able to perceive how we make a living as a vocation or a calling rather than simply as a job or work; and 3) believing in something larger, or higher, than ourselves. Conversely, there is no significant correlation between wealth, or health, or education, and authentic happiness.

These research results are very helpful to any coach working with clients to achieve their highest level goals. It is important for the coach to clarify, of course, which of the two realms of personality development the client falls under: social–cognitive maturity or social–emotional well-being.[116] That will largely explain the virtues held highest by that client, as well as what specific approaches to goal-directed tasks will be experienced as 'flow'.

The coach should also be alert to the following criteria for exploring his/her client's signature strengths. Observing for these criteria will bring into focus the client's truly innate strengths.

- Ownership – it is authentic
- Excitement when using it
- Rapid learning – it seems to come naturally
- Find new ways to use it
- Yearning to use it
- Inevitability – hard to keep from using it
- Feel invigorated and energized when using it

**Process for Reinforcing Strengths**

We include here a hypnotic process for a hypnosis-trained coach to use with clients in exploring their signature strengths. Coaches using this process should remember to treat shock if it emerges as well as allowing for cathartic release.

1. Client should identify their three strongest qualities from the *VIA Strengths* questionnaire.
2. Write them each on a separate card and discuss these with coach, selecting the one that seems to have the most conflicted energy around it.
3. **INDUCTION**: Coach will do an induction to facilitate the client going into a trance state.
4. "Now get in touch with these positive qualities." If necessary, the coach can remind the client of the three strongest qualities selected.
5. "Feel and experience the one you identified as having the most conflicted energy. Claim it as your natural gift or talent or quality."
6. **AGE REGRESSION**: "Now may I will tap you on the forehead? Go back to a time when as a child, you were displaying this natural quality and you were shamed or thwarted in your natural expression of it. Explore the details of this event. What are your feelings about this particular natural quality? How do you begin to behave regarding it?" Take as much time as your client needs. Remember that this is coaching, not therapy, so keep focused on the internal relationship to that natural quality rather than on the external relationship with the person who is shaming or thwarting them.
7. **CONCLUSION**: "What conclusion did you draw about yourself here? What were your behavioral decisions?"

8. "Now we will begin to reclaim this talent, gift or quality which you know has always been present for you and which you are now willing to claim as your own."

9. **ANCHORING**: "See, imagine or feel this natural quality as a symbol...what symbol comes to you that emanates the essence of this quality? Raise your finger when this is clear to you and tell me. I will write it on your card for you."

10. "Now discover a word or a phrase that will bring this quality clearly into your mind. Raise your finger when this comes to you and tell me."

11. "Now let a color come to you that enhances this quality and I will write it on the card for you."

12. **AGE REGRESSION**: "Now let yourself go to a time in your life when you clearly expressed this talent or gift with confidence; a time that was uncontaminated by someone else's negativity. When that comes, raise your finger. . . . Now tell me what it is and I will place this card in one hand as an anchor for these positive qualities."

13. **ANCHORING**: "Now see yourself expressing this natural gift that you have, clearly and freely. Let the symbol also come to you . . . now increase the intensity by bringing in your color and your word and your phrase."

14. "Bring in your spiritual connection" if that is appropriate for this particular client, "and know that that presence is always with you." The coach may want to elaborate, adding other signature strengths or other resources to intensify the anchoring.

15. **NEW CONCLUSION**: "What new conclusion and decisions do you want to create for yourself regarding this quality to replace the old ones?" You can remind the client what the old conclusion and decisions were.

16. "Now I will bring you back to the room with this newly claimed gift or talent to keep as a treasured aspect of your essence and to use as often as possible."

## 10. Vision

Planning and goal-setting are common activities for individuals who seek the assistance of a coach, but often they are unaware of the distinctly unique activity of visioning. Planning and goal-setting are usually rational, cognitive, left-brained activities, utilizing sequential logic and reality-testing. Planning and goal-setting take on a very different flavor when one allows the right brain to bring its intuitive creativity to bear. Once the reflection and mindfulness state is familiar and accessible, a coach can encourage clients to discover their Inner Visionary. This aspect of the individual's personality is always capable of defining his/her highest vision for the potential future self, and, importantly, committing to manifesting it. Without that commitment, energized by passion and fueled by known strengths, the visions are really only daydreams or fantasies.

Within the context of a supportive community, visioning can be a shared project through brainstorming, Master Minding, or creating vision boards or other representations of the evolving future self. It can be crucial to create ceremonies and rituals to act as anchoring reminders, to keep focused on the vision, and to discover steps which clearly lead to realizing the vision.

Establishing Master Mind groups, sometimes called Vision Enhancement groups, can be a powerful way to enhance the discovery of clients' clear life vision and maintain forward progress toward its realization. In this way clients have an investment in their own forward movement and that of their Master Mind members. When the roups are consistently holding the vision for each other, members support one another and develop group consciousness, avoiding authority projections and supporting independence.

### The Master Mind or Vision Enhancement Principle

Napoleon Hill studied the most successful people of his time, including Carnegie, Rockefeller, and distilled their secrets of success in a book titled *The Law of Success*.[117] Here we have excerpted some of his conclusions, and the 9 steps he advocated for utilizing the power of a group.

"The process of mind-blending here described as a Master Mind, may be likened to the act of one who connects many electric batteries to a single transmission wire, thereby 'stepping up' the power flowing over that line. Each mind, through the principle of mind chemistry, stimulates all the other minds in the group, until the mind energy thus becomes so great that it penetrates to and connects with the universal energy known as ether, which, in turn, touches every atom of the entire universe.

A Master Mind may be created through the bringing together or blending, in a spirit of perfect harmony, of two or more minds. Out of this harmonious blending of the chemistry of the mind creates a third mind which may be appropriated and used by one or all of the individual minds. This Master Mind will remain available as long as the friendly, harmonious alliance between the individual minds exists. It will disintegrate and all evidence of its former existence will disappear the moment the friendly alliance is broken."

According to Hill, the first step is to adopt a Definite Purpose as an objective to be attained by the alliance, choosing individual members whose education, experience and influence are such as to make them of the greatest value in achieving that purpose.

There isn't any use in forming a Master Mind Alliance just to have someone to chat with. It will soon play out if you don't have a strong motive behind it, and it's up to you to plant that motive in the minds of the group members.

Your allies for this group should be chosen for their ability to help you get to where you are going. Do not choose people simply because you know them and like them. I have found out by experience that merely because you like a person is no reason whatsoever to have him as a member of your economic Master Mind Alliance. It is all right to have such a person in your social or purely personal alliance, where his contribution may simply be this very friendship you appreciate.

You should make a careful analysis of your purpose and list the items you will need for its attainment and then systematically go about supplying the links with which to forge the chain. Each member of the alliance should make some definite, distinctive, unique contribution to the overall picture.

Establish a definite place where the members of the alliance will meet, have a definite plan, and arrange a definite time for the mutual discussion of the plan. You will recall the importance of a plan in connection with your Definite Major Purpose. Well, this is the time and place to reveal that plan to those who are your friends and harmonious associates, who will have a community of interest in the success of the venture. You may think your plan is very good, but before you get through discussing it with your allies you will undoubtedly modify it until you hit upon the perfect plan.

When you have established rapport between your mind ant he minds of others in your Master Mind Alliance, you will find that ideas will flow into the minds of each of the members and likewise into your own mind. When the Master Mind is in effect, it produces ideas that would not come to your mind alone. I have had that experience many times when sitting in on the many groups of which I am a member on a consulting basis.

The Round Table discussion will be the place where everyone meets, and where each member may speak with confidence. They all see what's on the table. You have no secrets in such a group, which results from the care with which you select members.

It is important that frequent and regular contacts be made between the members. Indefiniteness on this point, or utter neglect, will bring defeat. You must keep in almost continuous contact with the other minds of the group if you are to get the full benefit of them.

### Nine Steps into Group Empowerment utilizing the Master Mind Principle

(This is one possible formulation of the statement of these steps – the members of a Master Mind group may choose to reword them in a way that suits them as individuals.)

### I am Open

I admit that without a higher power, I am not as empowered to transform my challenges, and to improve my life. I now ask for help.

### I Believe

I am ready to be changed. I now affirm beliefs and attitudes that transform my life into my highest potential.

### I Decide to Be Changed
I make a decision to open my will and my life to my higher Self. I ask to be deeply healed and transformed so that I will be an instrument of love and compassion in the world.

### I Allow & I Trust
I realize that I now can allow my life to be supported by a Higher Plan and Power. I trust and allow divine guidance to touch me.

### I Ask
I now make known my specific requests, asking my partner's support, in knowing that higher mind, is fulfilling all my needs. (Each partner reads their written list of requests to the other members of the group, holding their palms outward to receive and give their energetic support to the manifesting of the member's requests).

### I Give Thanks
I give thanks that my Self is responding to my needs. I experience the emotional, holographic Gestalt of my requests being fulfilled now.

### I Dedicate My Life
I now have a covenant in which it is agreed that my Self is supplying me with an abundance of all things necessary and needed to live a successful and full life. I dedicate myself to be of service to the divine and all life, to live in a manner that sets the highest example for others to follow and to remain responsive to divine guidance.

### I Intend to Wake Up
I now intend to use all my will and effort to wake up from the sleep of my automatic, unconscious life. I now call upon all the forces available to assist me in this great work of spiritual awakening. I affirm that every day I make use of the tools for transformation available to me and I welcome each day with expectancy in giving me the chance to transform myself, my life and the world around me.

## I Actualize

I go forth now with a spirit of joy, excitement and expectancy, releasing all my cares and concerns. I give thanks and I am balanced, in harmony and equanimity.

As a coach, we help our clients to create visions of their Best Possible Future Self, a positive intervention familiar to many coaches.[118,119]

A great example is Benjamin Zander, the Principal Conductor of the Boston Philharmonic and teacher at the New England Conservatory of Music, who uses a variation of this principle which he calls "Giving an A."[120] At the beginning of each semester for his music students, he asks them to write a letter as if it's the end of the semester, beginning with "Dear Mr. Zander, I got my A because . . ." Several guidelines help this exercise to create possibility: it must be written in the past tense and it must tell the story in great detail, of not what they *did*, but what they *became* over the course of the semester to align who they are with the grade they received. The students are literally writing a new story for themselves—one from the point of view of a greater self, a best possible self, filled with the details of who that new self is.

Coaches might want to make use of exercises like this one to unleash the creative forces within their clients, and to proactively reinforce the steadfast pursuit of their own best possible future self.

Creating new visions of the possibilities that lie ahead begins with clarity about how our shadows, the remnants of the past that we still carry with us, affect our attitudes, beliefs, and behaviors today. So we make peace with our past, integrate the splintered parts of ourselves, and embrace the whole of who we are. In this way our present is no longer created by the momentum of our personal past. Now the work of being able to be a visionary can begin, to hold an untainted image of the possible, for yourself and for your community. The Sufis call it "unfurling the potential of being."[121]

We are all visionaries already, of course. We all create and hold images of the possible that become our reality tomorrow. Too often, though, the vision we hold is limited and contaminated, or it is a carbon copy of today due to a lack of creativity and openness to the new and unfamiliar. That is why it is so important to first confront and make allies of the guardians along the way, so that our new visions truly are new.

We must tap into the visionary energies available to us, and that requires sacrifice (making sacred). We sacrifice our fears of the unknown, we sacrifice our need to be in control and to know what is going to happen every step of the way. We sacrifice some degree of our comfort, which any journey requires. We sacrifice the reliance on our rational thinking to always make the best choices on our behalf, and begin to rely more on our intuition, and on the help being offered by angels and ancestors, spirit and nature guides.

Four universal human resources one needs to access in order to act creatively in this world are one's power, one's love, one's wisdom, and one's vision. Each resource has a shadow side, which must be acknowledged and dealt with as well.[122]

We may have already encountered the shadow sides of these resources.

1. The shadow side of power is addiction to intensity, to drama, to sensationalizing everything, and it may also be to dominate, manipulate, and control.
2. The shadow side of love is addiction to perfection. "I must be perfect. Everything around me must be perfect." And at bottom it is really "If I'm perfect enough, I'm going to get love."
3. The shadow side of wisdom is the addiction to the need to know before you step out. It's also a need to control, which comes from fear and lack of trust.
4. The shadow side of vision is an addiction to what doesn't work. There's always a "but." It is difficult to change from the old tried and true ways, even if they continually turn out to be not very true. This shadow visionary's sights are set on the past, limited to what has not worked.

Now there are two kinds of visions that we may discover when we open up to the possibilities.[123] *Interpretive spiritual experiences* are ordinary experiences that we might interpret spiritually, e.g., a beautiful sunset as evidence of God's love. *Visionary spiritual experiences* are dramatic, perceptual experiences involving spirit realities e.g., mystical experiences, seeing a ghost, feeling attacked by an evil spirit, a near-death experience, or experiencing a visit from a deceased loved one. So to experience visions, to access visionary energies, we must be open to what is invisible to the eye and beyond the comprehension of the everyday mind. And for most of us that means entering altered states of consciousness where we are suspended at the threshold between everyday consciousness and dream sleep. We reach this state through hypnosis or trance, prayer or meditation. We could call this a state of reverie.

Open yourself to what is invisible to the eye and beyond the comprehension of the everyday mind. When you are open to it, you may journey to and *access other non-physical worlds*; you may make contact with *non-material, normally invisible, spirit beings* in the form of ancestors, animals, plants, or certain places such as a river, cave, or rainforest. This contact may provide you with *access to hidden knowledge.*[124]

One ancient model of how to take such a journey is the *vision quest*, an initiation ritual designed to move an adult into a new stage in his life with a sense of direction and purpose. A vision can take the appearance of an animal, a shape in a cloud, a synchronistic event. If the meaning of the vision is not immediately clear to one's left brain, the right is capable of understanding. Be open to being shown a whole world that parallels this one. Know that you can derive strength and information here, and that you may be called to make sacrifices. Also, be open to accepting gifts, gratefully.

In a state of reverie, the door is open between the collective unconscious and personal conscious. One is suspended at the threshold between day consciousness and dream sleep. At this threshold many otherwise impossible things become reality.

Allow yourself to enter this magical threshold, and experience visions of your own. As a coach, be willing to facilitate your clients' journeys to and beyond this threshold where they may find answers to questions and solutions to dilemmas that are not available in any other way. And so we present here the Inner Visionary Process.

## Meeting Your Inner Visionary Process

This is a guided visualization that you can do for a client, or for a group of clients. Have your client declare an *intention* for the journey (such as "I want to be more clear about the direction of my life" or "I want to be more open and less defended in all my relationships") and formulate one or more *questions to ask* (such as, "What teacher or teachings should I be following spiritually?" or "How can I become more disciplined in the choices I make each day?").

This guided visualization can be facilitated within the context of a hypnotic trance or simply in a quiet relaxed state. If the coach is trained in hypnosis, and if the client is open to using it, we suggest this process will be significantly enhanced by using hypnosis. Therefore, the coach who is utilizing hypnosis for this process will begin with an induction of his/her choice. In either case providing soft lighting and inspirational soft 'hypnotic' or 'massage' music will deepen the client's access to the unconscious.

1.  "There is a path emerging near you in your nature place which winds towards the horizon. It is a beautiful clear path. See or experience yourself walking along this path. This is a journey within yourself to a place that lies beyond the guardians, and you are confident in moving forward because you know these guardians well, and they are now your allies in the journey. One by one, allow yourself to encounter the guardians from the six realms, and to remind yourself of the strength that each one carries for you. Invite them to accompany you as you continue this journey toward the treasure that will be yours when you find it and claim it to be your own. . . *(pause)* . . .

2.  "Now allow yourself to see or experience an entry into the earth that feels familiar and safe to you. It may even appear as someplace you know in ordinary reality. This opening might be a cave, well, spring, hollow tree, sweat lodge or any opening that holds some particular fascination or where you intuitively sense spiritual energy. The opening can be anywhere and any size. . . .

*(pause)* . . . When you are ready to enter the opening, immediately you find yourself in a tunnel, hallway, or chute that feels very inviting. Using all your senses, be fully present here. Make your way to the end of the tunnel or hallway, where you find a doorway. It may look whimsical or stately, but in any case it leads to a magical realm. When you have entered through the door, allow yourself to explore the landscape in detail. When you are ready, voice your intention, knowing that your Inner Visionary will make an appearance. Be open to any form that it may take, however; he/she may appear as a human, an animal or bird, as a book or an altar or something from nature like a tree, flower or an invisible force like the wind. . . . *(pause)* . . . Quietly get to know this visionary – "What is your name?", "How old are you?", "Which moments in my life are the most important highlights to you?", "What are your favorite things for me to do?" When you are ready, raise your finger and share your experience with your partner. . . . *(pause)* . . .

3.  "Now you must become aware that this is an initiation you are being asked to undertake in order to receive clear messages and a clear vision. There is always a sacrifice required in every initiation. Just as the guardians along your path were necessary to strengthen you for this journey, so the sacrifices are required to strengthen you and to build fortitude for your vision. Be very still, open and receptive. What can you do, what qualities can you embrace to sanctify this meeting with the Visionary? Perhaps you will need to find within yourself the quality of patience – is it difficult for you to slow down and be still? Perhaps you will need to humble yourself, crying out for a vision – is it difficult for you to ask for help? What is the sacrifice that you must make if you are to receive a vision? To give up your belief about how things "should be"? To be willing to question what you have always accepted about the limitations in your life? To accept a vision that may require you to make major lifestyle changes? What is the sacrifice that you must make if you are to receive a vision in this

initiation? . . . *(pause)* . . . When you are clear about
what the sacrifices are, commit to yourself and to your
Inner Visionary that you are ready to make them. If you
are clear that a particular sacrifice is required, but you
feel you are unwilling or unable to commit to it,
acknowledge this now. And know that the vision you are
about to receive will be modified accordingly. . . .
*(pause)* . . .

4.  "Now you may ask the questions you came to ask,
    knowing that your Inner Visionary will speak only truth
    to you. Other questions may arise in your awareness as
    well. You can ask all the questions that you want to, as
    long as your Inner Visionary is willing. . . . *(pause)* . . .
    When you have received your answers, make an
    agreement that you will be able to meet again, and agree
    on a ritual through which that meeting can easily happen
    when you want it to. . . . *(pause)* . . .

5.  "It is time to say goodbye to your Inner Visionary for
    now, to leave this magical realm that you are in, and to
    return back to your everyday life. The return is along the
    same path as the descent but your pace can be quicker
    now as you feel excitement and energy flowing through
    you. Return through the doorway, entering the tunnel or
    hallway. Notice any details about this place, making a
    mental note to record in memory. This helps to make
    this place more familiar, and easier to return to at
    another time. Now travel through the tunnel or hallway
    until you get to the other end of it, and to the opening
    which takes you back up to the everyday world. Really
    be with the feelings of being here at the bottom of this
    opening, looking up at the other world. Remind yourself
    of the sacrifices you are committed to making when you
    return to your life there. And when you are ready, climb
    up out of the opening into the earth, and feel the
    sunshine and the refreshing breeze. . . . *(pause)* . . .

6.  "Let yourself experience the excitement of your new
    discovery with all your senses, with all your being.
    Embrace this new self, this possible self you are now
    becoming, open to the visionary within. Even though
    you don't fully understand the vision yet, express your

gratitude for it. Express your intention to keep it in the foreground of your awareness over the coming days and weeks, to honor the vision and your Inner Visionary by setting aside time to ponder these things, to meditate and pray, to invest some time in reverie. . . . *(pause)* . . .

7. "You are now returning from your adventure to where you started. Soon you will be coming back to your waking consciousness, bringing this awareness back with you. You bring with you the newly revitalized visionary part of yourself. And you will find that any time you want to, it will be possible for you to get in touch with this expanded sense of yourself by simply closing your eyes for a moment, evoking the image or feeling you have right now, and reminding yourself that you have within you all the resources that you really need.

8. "Bring your attention and your hand to your Heart-Center. Experience this as the place of unconditional love within you. Know that there is an infinite supply of this love and that it is always there. Feel it like a bright warm sunshine within you, radiating light throughout you body. (*Pause*) . . . Now when you are ready, allow yourself to come back to the room, back into your body."

9. *(Five count wake up).*

Allow your client(s) some quiet time to reflect on the experience and to complete the following worksheet. You may want to leave the music on to encourage continuing in the quiet mindful state.

You may want to record the client's responses to the process on the following Worksheet as you facilitate it for him/her. Or you can ask the client to complete the Worksheet after reflection on the experience.

## Meeting Your Inner Visionary Worksheet

My *intention* for the journey:

_____

_____

_____

_____

_____

The *questions I want to ask* my Inner Visionary:

_____

_____

_____

_____

Description of the opening, tunnel, doorway, and the magical realm: _____

_____

_____

_____

What I learn about the visionary:

_____

_____

_____

_____

_____

_____

The sacrifices I must make:

_____

_____

_____

_____

_____

_____

Answers to my questions:

_____

_____

_____

_____

_____

_____

_____

_____

Agreements to meet again:

_____

_____

_____

_____

_____

_____

## 11. Life Transitions

Coaching clients often request the help of a coach at times in their life that are turning points. They may be leaving an employment position, or stepping out of a career, or advancing into a promotion, or entering a new primary relationship. Transitions are those unique times when we leave the old but have not yet stepped into the new. They can be an exciting and invigorating part of life, yet transitions can also be stressful, even happy ones.

Coaches may want to incorporate a Life Stress assessment into their initial intake information with new clients. Here is the Holmes and Rahe Stress Scale, constructed in 1967 by psychiatrists Thomas Holmes and Richard Rahe.[125]

### Stressfulness of Life Events

| Life event | Life change units |
| --- | --- |
| Death of a spouse | 100 |
| Divorce | 73 |
| Marital separation | 65 |
| Imprisonment | 63 |
| Death of a close family member | 63 |
| Personal injury or illness | 53 |
| Marriage | 50 |
| Dismissal from work | 47 |
| Marital reconciliation | 45 |
| Retirement | 45 |
| Change in health of family member | 44 |
| Pregnancy | 40 |
| Sexual difficulties | 39 |
| Gain a new family member | 39 |
| Business readjustment | 39 |
| Change in financial state | 38 |
| Death of a close friend | 37 |
| Change to different line of work | 36 |
| Change in frequency of arguments | 35 |

| Life event | Life change units |
|---|---|
| Major mortgage | 32 |
| Foreclosure of mortgage or loan | 30 |
| Change in responsibilities at work | 29 |
| Child leaving home | 29 |
| Trouble with in-laws | 29 |
| Outstanding personal achievement | 28 |
| Spouse starts or stops work | 26 |
| Beginning or end school | 26 |
| Change in living conditions | 25 |
| Revision of personal habits | 24 |
| Trouble with boss | 23 |
| Change in working hours or conditions | 20 |
| Change in residence | 20 |
| Change in schools | 20 |
| Change in recreation | 19 |
| Change in church activities | 19 |
| Change in social activities | 18 |
| Minor mortgage or loan | 17 |
| Change in sleeping habits | 16 |
| Change in number of family reunions | 15 |
| Change in eating habits | 15 |
| Vacation | 13 |
| Christmas | 12 |
| Minor violation of law | 11 |

**Score of 300+**: At risk of illness.
**Score of 150-299**: Risk of illness is moderate (reduced by 30% from the above risk).
**Score <150**: Only have a slight risk of illness.

While the circumstances of major life stress are always different, the skills and attitudes needed to successfully move ahead are always the same, namely being positive, patient, and proactive. The coach working with an individual in the midst of such challenging changes in his/her life will want to address them directly.

To the extent that clients identify or define themselves by their surroundings, lifestyle, roles or external validation, such major changes can be disorienting and disturbing. This can cause self-doubt, anxiety and confusion as new circumstances are adjusted to and a new "normal" is reestablished.

Coaches will certainly be aware of the wonderful opportunities for growth that transition present. It is a natural time to take a look at how you can bring those parts of yourself that you most value into your new role, and just as important, to leave behind the areas of yourself that you'd like to make changes to.

Here may be a perfect opportunity for the hypnosis-trained coach to utilize the technique to help the client go back in age regression to times in their life when they dealt successfully with transitions. What helped you get through that period in your life, and what would you have done differently?

Needless to say, part of what helps one feel secure in transition is having a healthy support system. Encourage the client to stay connected with his/her Master Mind group and other support. We will discuss the Master Mind principle in the next section.

## 12. Mastery Plan

The coach is always oriented toward creating a **Life Mastery Plan** with results that are attainable, measurable, specific and have target dates for achievement. And toward tangible steps that will lead to its attainment. The coach encourages and motivates the client to change whatever behaviors are obstacles, any of those shadow self-defeating patterns in the client's life. Focusing on the potential "best possible future self", a Behavior Change Agreement may need to be negotiated between all "selves", i.e., shadows and resources, to insure the plan's implementation. The Plan certainly must identify and access all relevant resources, including personal strengths and a personal support system. Having the Plan be measurable and including target dates for achievement allows the coach to assist the client in tracking successes, and also the accountability necessary to know when and how to course correct. Sometimes the identified steps need to be adjusted, rearranged, or discarded. And finally, the coach keeps the client accountable and on track between sessions through assignments and check-ins.

## Your Life Mastery Plan Process

This process is one that accesses the client's deep unconscious to begin answering the existential question "What is your Soul's purpose at this time on earth?" The coach prepares the client to make the most of this process by providing a dimly lit room with quiet background music and the expectation that it will actually produce a **Life Mastery Plan.**

1. The client responds to these three questions with single word answers, spontaneously with no thought or censoring:
    a. "What do you want?" Write answer in first column of the worksheet.
    b. "What means will you use to get this?" Write answer in second column.
    c. "What experience are you looking for?" Write answer in third column.
2. Continue this process for 5 minutes, repeating the questions slowly and recording the answers exactly without comments.
3. Now allow the client to review his/her answers recorded on the worksheet.
4. Instruct the client, "Focusing on your responses to question 3 ('What experience are you looking for?') write down the words that seem to be repeated the most and that seem most attractive and activating to you."
5. "Now put the words together and come up with a one sentence statement, which includes as much of the content as possible. This statement should be brief enough to easily recall anytime, anywhere. This is your *Purpose Statement*, or statement of *How I Best Express My Essence*."
6. This Purpose statement should be reviewed often and be at the top of every Master Mind process. It should be on the tip of your tongue whenever someone asks, "What's most important to you in your life?" or "What is your life purpose?"

7. "Now use the worksheet to identify any *negative support* you have in your life to keep you from progressing on fulfilling your life purpose.
   a. List the people and activities that seem to drain your energy, time and resources.
   b. List the time-wasting activities that sidetrack or sabotage you.
   c. List the people who really do not want to see you achieve your goals.
   d. List the old infantile self-limiting beliefs about yourself that still seem to be holding you back.
8. "Now use the worksheet to identify any *positive support* you have to encourage you to fulfill your life purpose."
   a. List the people and activities that support your personal growth, feed your soul and increase or have the potential to increase your resources.
   b. Write out your new beliefs about yourself that support your life purpose goals.
9. "Write 5 clear goals that will lead you to your life's purpose this year." (These can be reviewed each year)
   a. If a goal is completed, then add another goal for the New Year.
   b. If not completed, re-evaluate whether to continue with it, revise it, or delete it.
   c. New goals may be added, not to exceed five total goals each year.
10. "Write a **Year-long Action Plan**, with definite time frames and deadlines, that supports your five clear goals for this year."
   a. List the steps that you need to take to get you there this year.
   b. Identify three of these steps per week as your weekly goals.
   c. Ask for the support of your Master Mind group in achieving these 3 goals each week.
   d. Ask for brainstorming if you get stuck.
   e. At the beginning of each Master Mind meeting, repeat your **Life Purpose Statement**, your five clear **yearly goals** and your **Action Plan** statement.

## Your Life Mastery Plan Worksheet

| 1. What do you want? | 2. How will you get it? | 3. What experience are you looking for? |
| --- | --- | --- |
| _____ | _____ | _____ |
| _____ | _____ | _____ |
| _____ | _____ | _____ |
| _____ | _____ | _____ |
| _____ | _____ | _____ |
| _____ | _____ | _____ |
| _____ | _____ | _____ |
| _____ | _____ | _____ |
| _____ | _____ | _____ |
| _____ | _____ | _____ |
| _____ | _____ | _____ |
| _____ | _____ | _____ |
| _____ | _____ | _____ |
| _____ | _____ | _____ |

Purpose statement:

_____

_____

_____

_____

Drains on your energy, time and resources:

_____

_____

_____

Time-wasting activities that sidetrack or sabotage you:

_____

_____

_____

People who really do not want to see you achieve your goals:

_____

_____

_____

Self-limiting beliefs about yourself that are holding you back:

_____

_____

_____

People and activities that support your personal growth, feed your soul, and increase or have the potential to increase your resources:

_____

_____

_____

Your new beliefs about yourself that support your life purpose:

_____

_____

_____

**5 clear goals** that will lead you to your life's purpose <u>this year</u>:

1. _____

   _____

2. _____

   _____

3. _____

   _____

4. _____

   _____

5. _____

   _____


**Year-long Action Plan**

_____

_____

_____

_____


**Three steps for *this week***

_____

_____

_____

_____

### 13. Ethics of personal coaching

Many but not all of the same ethical considerations apply to coaching as to psychotherapy. Confidentiality is vital to establishing and keeping the confidence and trust of the client. The coach must always be following the client's agenda, not the coach's, guided by the question "How does *the client* define success?" Ethically, it is the client's responsibility not only to determine the direction of the shared work, but to be accountable for the results. Coaches must be cautious to maintain clear well-defined boundaries with their clients, always avoiding dual relationships. The professional needs to identify his/her role with the client as either therapist or coach. Serving both roles simultaneously is a prohibited dual relationship.

While there are directional and inspirational aspects of leadership in the coaching relationship, serving as a spiritual guide or teacher and as a coach simultaneously is a prohibited dual relationship unless it was explicitly stated to be incorporated in the initial coaching agreement.

The Code of Ethics for Board Certified Coaches (through the Center for Credentialing and Certification) includes the following:

### PERFORMANCE OF SERVICES

Board Certified Coaches shall:
1. Conduct all occupational activities in a responsible manner.
2. Recognize the limitations of coaching practice and qualifications, and provide services only when qualified. Coaches are responsible for determining the limits of their competency based on education, knowledge, skills, experience, credentials and other relevant considerations.
3. Protect the privacy of information obtained in the course of providing services, including electronic files and communications. Coaches shall not disclose this information unless authorized to do so by applicable legal requirements, client authorization or the written coaching agreement. The limits of privacy shall be clearly identified before coaching services begin.
4. Properly use occupational credentials, titles and degrees; and provide accurate information concerning education,

experience, qualifications and the performance of services.

5. Avoid coaching techniques that are harmful or have been shown to be ineffective. Coaches are responsible for ensuring that the techniques used are consistent with clients' emotional, intellectual and physical needs. Coaches shall inform clients regarding the purpose, application and results of the techniques, assessments and strategies.

6. Obtain a written coaching service agreement before initiating a coaching relationship. This agreement shall include the rights, roles and responsibilities of the parties involved, as well as the manner in which private information will be protected.

7. Seek supervision from qualified professionals when necessary, and provide referrals when unable to provide appropriate assistance to a client as well as when terminating a service relationship.

8. Ensure that clients, sponsors and colleagues understand that coaching services are not counseling, therapy or psychotherapy services, and avoid providing counseling, therapy and psychotherapy.

## AVOIDANCE OF CONFLICTS OF INTEREST
Board Certified Coaches shall:

1. Disclose to others, including sponsors, clients or colleagues, significant circumstances that could be construed as a potential or real conflict of interest, or any having an appearance of impropriety.

2. Avoid conduct that could cause a conflict of interest regarding clients or sponsors. If a conflict of interest occurs, coaches shall take reasonable steps to resolve the conflict.

3. Avoid engaging in multiple relationships with clients or sponsors. In situations where multiple relationships cannot be avoided, coaches shall discuss the potential effects of the relationships with the affected individuals and shall take reasonable steps to avoid any harm. This discussion should also be noted in the client's record.

4. Avoid sexual or romantic relationships with current clients. Coaches shall not engage in sexual or romantic interactions with former clients for a minimum of two (2) years following the date of termination.
5. Refrain from offering or accepting significant payments, gifts or other forms of compensation or benefits outside of the written coaching service agreement.
6. Acknowledge accurately the intellectual property of others with respect to all activities.

Let's address a variety of ethics topics more specifically. The field of coaching is relatively new and unregulated, making the need for a clear set of guiding principles even more necessary for the practitioner coach.

### Informed consent

Informed consent is a principle of ethical coaching based on the core value of self-determination. It is a basic value in the helping professions that the individual has the right to determine for him/ herself the kind of help they receive, and indeed whether they participate at all. The individual requires, and deserves to have, adequate information to fully assess whether and how they wish to participate in coaching. Informed consent minimally should include a discussion of financial issues and the basic nature of the services that are and are not provided. It should address confidentiality and privacy issues. Informed consent is only possible when consent is given voluntarily by a person of legal age, mentally competent to refuse or consent, based on sufficiently thorough and accurate information in order to weigh the benefits and risks of treatment. The following categories of information should be included in initial intake paperwork, and easily available to clients.

1) **Confidentiality**. By openly addressing confidentiality issues during the informed consent process, and over time as they are relevant, the coach develops a collaborative relationship with the client that is based on trust and an understanding of the parameters of the professional relationship. Confidentiality might include such measures as sound proofing the office, storing treatment records in a secure location, using passwords

and other security measures with computers, and not discussing confidential information in public or with unauthorized people.

2) **Clear disclosure of one's training and experience** is a basic requirement of any professional. It is unethical to embellish or otherwise falsify one's education, experience history, or qualifications whether it be with clients, third-party payers, or colleagues.

3) **Spirituality and religion**. Include questions about spirituality and religion in the initial intake paperwork for each client. This establishes as part of the informed consent that these issues are appropriate to be included in the coaching experience. Unless the coaching practice is clearly established as representing a parochial religious or spiritual point of view, inclusion of these issues should be generic and the coach needs to carefully avoid allowing his/her own beliefs to contaminate the clients' resolution of any spiritual struggles.

4) **Fees and policies regarding fees** need to be stated clearly at the outset. In fact, it may be very helpful to discuss these issues in the initial telephone contact even before actually meeting. For many clients knowing the fees charged for coaching, expectations for when payment is due, if credit cards are accepted and related financial details, can impact an individual's decision to enter coaching. Provide a clear policy on missed appointment and late cancellation charges. This policy should be reviewed in the informed consent process. The policy used should be clear and fair.

5) **Conflicts of interest**. Informing clients of potential or actual conflicts of interest, such as financial interest in certain procedures, products or referrals, or religious interest in persuading a client to decide against abortion or divorce. A conflict of interest exists when the coach's personal, scientific, professional, legal, financial, or other interests or relationships impair their objectivity with the client, or when it may expose the client to harm or exploitation.

When coaches provide services to two or more people who have a relationship with each other (for example, family members or staff members of an agency), they should clarify with all parties which individuals will be considered clients and the nature of the coach's professional obligations to the various individuals who are receiving services.

## Competence

It is the coaching professionals' responsibility to represent themselves and to practice only within the boundaries of their education, experience, training, licensure or certification, and level of supervisory or consultant support.

One should refrain from making false, misleading, deceptive or unsubstantiated claims or statements in resumes, advertising and other means of soliciting clients. One needs to avoid setting unrealistic expectations for a prospective client in order to attract them to become a paying client. In other words, the professional must not inflate their own competencies, nor those of the coaching modality to be offered.

## Dual Relationships

Dual relationships are defined as engaging in the coaching relationship as well as one or more additional relationships with that individual or one related to, or closely associated with, the client. These might include other relationships that are social, business, sexual, or others. The overriding criteria for appropriateness of these dual relationships is whether the client is potentially being exploited through the imbalance of power that automatically exists within your coach-client relationship. In any case, the coach is responsible for setting and communicating clear, appropriate, and culturally sensitive boundaries with the client. The parameters of what constitutes appropriate dual relationships in coaching are certainly more relaxed than in psychotherapy, as the coaching relationship is predominantly one falling under a business model rather than a medical model.

## Self-care

A coach's self-care program may include the use of personal psychotherapy, a peer supervision or support group, limiting the number of hours one works, taking time for personal pursuits and relationships, taking regular breaks from work and vacations, ensuring adequate diet, sleep and exercise, engaging in enjoyable activities and hobbies, varying one's work activities, and striking a balance between different professional and personal activities over time (Sarnel & Barnett, 1998). It is a clear and overt value within the Wellness community that we all benefit from continued emotional healing and personal growth; transformational psychotherapy is a lifelong endeavor, and the best defense against professional distress, burnout, compassion fatigue, and impairment.

**Fees**

When deciding to raise one's fees during the course of a coaching engagement, adequate notice should be given and each client's ability to pay the higher fee should be discussed. One option is to increase one's fees for new referrals and keep the fees for current clients the same. Then, over time all clients will be paying the higher fee and the issue of creating a hardship for current clients will be avoided.

Address the issue of fees as early as is feasible in a professional coaching relationship. Since this is something that could impact the client's willingness and ability to participate in coaching, such issues should always be discussed during the informed consent process. A clear policy on missed appointment and late cancellation charges should be reviewed in the informed consent process.

While the use of a collection agency is allowable, establishing a policy for a maximum outstanding balance allowed and including this in the informed consent agreement may be a better course of action. Then, if for any reason the balance owed comes to this amount the coach should further discuss this with the client, see what options exist, and then proceed accordingly. Possible options include meeting less frequently for a period of time, use of a payment plan, reducing one's fee, providing a limited number of pro bono sessions or a referral to a provider or organization with a sliding scale or reduced fee structure.

### Availability

Coaches should have a clear policy regarding if, when and how they are available to their clients outside the scheduled appointment times. Generally this would occur through email and if so, state what is the response time that the client can expect.

### Confidentiality

As coaches, we do our best to treat information shared by clients as confidential within the context of a business relationship, and not to the standard demanded in a psychotherapeutic or medical context.

### Multicultural competence

Cultural competence can be applied to all individuals because everyone has a culture and is part of several subcultures, including those related to age, ethnicity, gender, sexual orientation, race, religion/spirituality, national origin, socioeconomic status, language preference, ideology, geographic region, neighborhood, physical ability/disability and others. Coaches cannot be expected to know everything about every group, but we can have an awareness of the importance of the multiple aspects of diversity addressed above.

### Self-disclosure

The appropriate use of self-disclosure by the coach may be a very useful and powerful technique when it is done for the client's benefit within the context of the coaching process. Used as a tool to instruct or illustrate, the coach's disclosure of some past event or problem can help the client overcome barriers to progress toward stated goals. The self-disclosure should never occur to meet the clinician's needs for intimacy or other personal needs.

### Integrating spirituality and religion into coaching practice

Recent studies have demonstrated that there is a positive link between religion/spirituality and health and wellbeing.[126] Therefore dealing with these aspects of a client's life may be important or even crucial to advancing the goals established in the initial coaching agreement. Clearly, a coach should not impose their own values and beliefs on clients or overstep their role by espousing ecclesiastical authority.

## Terminating the coaching engagement

If it is clear that the patient is not benefiting from coaching, we have ethical responsibilities to terminate appropriately. The coach should assert his/her ethical responsibility (and right) to terminate the engagement with any appropriate referral.

Eventual termination is an important part of the coaching process. At the beginning of coaching, and throughout the engagement, we have responsibilities to provide informed consent about the process of coaching, including the factors involved in deciding when to stop.

A key strategy is to explicitly review the presenting concerns, goals and progress from time to time with the client. This helps clarify how much has been accomplished, as well as what still needs to be addressed and whether the client and coach collaboratively wish to continue or not.

## Working with non-ordinary states of consciousness

When utilizing hypnosis or similar trance states in the coaching intervention, provide some description about the phenomenon of hypnosis that reflects your theoretical orientation, and this should be included in the initial informed consent materials. According to the American Society of Clinical Hypnosis[127], this might include such topics as (a) what it consists of, (b) how it is a frequently occurring state for some (like watching a movie, or a football game, etc.), (c) how it could be a natural coping mechanism for some, such as in dealing with emergency situations, or (d) that it can also happen spontaneously for some (highway hypnosis). Hypnosis could also be described as facilitating the development of new skills, behaviors, and thought patterns to be used in place of maladaptive ones, and that further practice strengthens the new learning. Also discuss the common fears - losing control, losing consciousness, risking being "trapped" in hypnosis, etc. Also, it could be emphasized that the individual can leave hypnosis at any point (like turning off a television set.

When the professional incorporates hypnotic experience in any group or public presentation, he/she needs to take care to ensure that it is done in such a way as to prevent or minimize risk to unknown audience participants. This might be accomplished by, for example, telling those who do not wish to go into hypnosis not to close their eyes, or by muting the induction part of a demonstration video.

# Chapter Three
# Approaches to Coaching

Coaching can be defined in numerous ways because there are many diverse approaches within the field. This is just as true as it is for the field of psychotherapy. We use the definition that coaching is an approach to helping people increase their sense of self-direction, self-esteem, efficacy and achievement.[128] Mentoring is basically the same process, but mentoring relies on the specific experience and knowledge of the mentor/coach being greater than that of the client. An effective coach may not know more than his/her client in specific areas of competence, but does provide value added in how to approach, organize, and implement a path to achieving the client's goals. In other words, one need not be an expert in the law to be an effective coach for an attorney.

One paradigm for categorizing approaches to coaching recognizes two distinctly different types of coaching: *skills coaching* and *transformational coaching*.[129,130,131] Skills coaching is directed at improving a coachees' skills or competencies, whereas transformational coaching aims to help coachees' achieve change by shifting to a higher level of functioning by changing habitual responses to issues.[132]

**Skills coaching** is directed at helping a coachee to develop their skills and competencies in order to improve their effectiveness in their current role. It tends to be didactic – does not specifically examine a coachee's underlying beliefs, attitudes and emotional reactions to a situation.

**Transformational coaching** is directed at helping a coachee to experience a 'felt shift', where they start to think, feel and act differently. It involves exploration of the beliefs, attitudes and emotional reactions underlying the coachees' habitual way of responding to situations, and tends to explore the values and life vision of the client.

Yossi Ives[133] proposes three dimensions across which to define coaching approaches: 1) Directive or non-directive; 2) Personal-developmental or goal-focused; and 3) therapeutic or performance-driven. He uses these distinctions to assess the following approaches to coaching, which were in turn brought together by Stober and Grant.[134]

- *Coaching from a humanist perspective* – Based on Rogerian[135,136] person-centered principles, it views positive change and self actualization as a driving force in the human psyche. Coaching from this point of view capitalizes on a person's inherent tendency to self-actualize and looks to stimulate a person's inherent growth potential. This approach draws from psychotherapy a strong emphasis on the practitioner-client relationship, suggesting that the relationship itself (its warmth and positive regard) is a main ingredient for growth. It also promotes a holistic approach, requiring the coach to address all aspects of the person.

- *Behavior based approach* - Peterson[137] advocates a behavioral approach that acknowledges the complexity of both the human being and her environment, but which nevertheless focuses on facilitating practical change over psychological adjustments. This approach is action focused insofar as it looks to the future and seeks to create change and imbed it in real life contexts.

- *Adult-development approach* – This approach is based on constructive-developmental theories: that as people develop they become more aware of and open to a mature understanding of authority and responsibility, and display greater tolerance of ambiguity. Coaching from this perspective is predicated upon the idea of four main stages of development and it suggests that coaching at each stage needs to focus on stage-of-development related issues.[138]

- *Cognitive coaching* – Auerbach[139] claims that although coaching must address the multiple facets of the individual, it is primarily a cognitive method. Fundamental to cognitive coaching is the view that one's feelings and emotions are the product of one's thoughts: a person's perceptions, interpretations, mental attitudes and beliefs. Cognitive therapy helps clients replace maladaptive and inaccurate cognitions.[140,141] Auerbach argues that a primary function of the coach is to assist the client in challenging and overcoming their maladaptive and distorted perceptions.

- *Adult learning approach* – This approach seeks to use coaching to stimulate deep learning. It draws from a range of adult-learning theories, such as andragogy[142], reflective practice[143], and experiential learning[144], which collectively argue that adults learn by reflecting on experiences. Cox[145] argues that, similarly, coaching can be seen as a learning approach designed to nurture goal-focused, self-directed learners who draw on their reservoir of previous experience with a view to solving real-life dilemmas. Gray (2005) advocates a transformative learning coaching model that seeks to raise the coachee's critical reflection to question assumptions. He suggests that coaching has become a tool in the increasing shift towards informal, self-directed learning in organisations.

- *Positive psychology model* – Kauffman[146] argues that coaching should work to identify and build on the client's strengths and should seek to engender hope and happiness. Positive psychology seeks to encourage people to look to what is good and going well in their lives to reinforce a positive disposition. Positive emotions, it is argued, widens a person's focus of attention and broadens access to the person's intellectual and psychological resources, resulting in improved performance. While certain aspects of the positive coaching model can be utilised to better achieve specific goals, it would seem it is primarily designed to effect general enhancement and life balance. Neenan and Dryden's *Life Coaching*[147] is entirely based on positive psychology and focuses on changing perceptions and attitudes.

- *An adventure-based model* – According to Kemp[148] adventure education is an appropriate conception of coaching, as both seek to press the boundaries and explore new frontiers and horizons. Both, he argues, begin with an analysis of the present state, set out a desired destination and develop the means of reaching it. Both involve a willingness to accept a measure of risk and uncertainty (with coaching: psychological injury), to move to the edge of their physical or psychological comfort zone – and that it is out of this risk that personal growth occurs. Kemp argues that adventure-based coaching asks the participant to test his cognitive, behavioural and emotional competence, and to effect change by formulating new behavioural responses to situations. Adventure is a process rather than an activity.[149] The learning attained during the adventure is captured or anchored and the lessons are later applied in real life settings.

- *Systemic approach* – Coaching using a systemic framework is about helping the client to recognize hitherto unrecognized patterns of behavior and forms of feedback, and in so doing to see their experiences in new ways. It also encourages a holistic view, in which various other parts of the system may have relevance to the issue at hand. Humans are complex adaptive systems insofar as they consist of a combination of interacting systems that are affected by change and can respond to changed circumstances. A systemic coaching model seeks to foreground complexity, unpredictability and contextual factors, and highlights the importance of small changes; it encourages openness, growth and creativity. This approach views the balance between stability and instability as optimal for performance.[150]

- *Goal-oriented approach* – The foregoing approaches may be contrasted with a strict goal-focused or solution-driven approach which sees the primary function of coaching fostering the client's self-regulation. According to Grant[151], "Coaching is essentially about helping individuals regulate and direct their interpersonal and intrapersonal resources to better attain their goals." The primary method is assisting the client to identify and form well crafted goals and develop an effective action plan. The role of the coach is to stimulate ideas and action and to ensure that the goals are consistent with the client's main life values an interests, rather than working on helping the client to adjust her values and beliefs. In this conception, coaching is essentially about raising performance and supporting effective action, rather than addressing feelings and thoughts, which it is thought will be indirectly addressed through actual positive results.[152] This type of approach is sometimes called 'brief coaching'[153] as it aims to achieve its goals in a comparatively short space of time and normally focusing on a relatively defined issue or goal.

| Type of coaching | Objective of coaching |
| --- | --- |
| Humanist | "Coaching is above all about human growth and change" (Stober, 2006, p. 17) |
| Behaviorist | "The purpose of coaching is to change behaviour" (Peterson, 2006, p.51) |
| Adult development | Coaching is about helping clients develop and grow in maturity |
| Cognitive coaching | Coaching is foremost about developing adaptive thoughts |
| Adult learning | A learning approach that helps self-directed learners to reflect on and grow from their experiences |
| Positive psychology approach | "Shift attention away from what causes and drives pain to what energizes and pulls people forward" (Kauffman, 2006, p. 220) |
| Adventure coaching | Stretching the client through entering into challenging situations and the learning that arises. |
| Systemic coaching | "Coaching is a journey in search of patterns" (Cavanagh, 2006, p. 313) |
| Goal-focused | "Coaching is a goal-oriented, solution-focused process" (Grant, 2006, p. 156) |

**Approaches to Coaching Chart**
[Quotes selected from Stober & Grant (2006)]

The following two approaches to coaching do not easily fall into the categories established by Sober and Grant.

- *Integrative Goal-Focused approach* – A goal-focused approach to coaching emphasizes the clients' self-regulation through setting a goal, developing a plan of action, beginning action, monitoring their performance, evaluating their performance by comparison to a standard, and changing their actions based on this evaluation to further enhance their performance and better reach their goals. The coach's role is to facilitate the client's movement through the self-regulatory cycle.[154]

- *Psychoanalytically Informed approach* – Accepting that the coaching relationship itself is largely the vehicle for clarification, motivation and action, psychoanalytically informed coaching emphasizes the subjective, out-of-awareness, unconscious, and very often hard-to-discuss aspects of the coach-client relationship. The coach assists the client to recognize more clearly how his/her internal world of attachments and emotional investments affects all decisions in life.[155] Actually, most coaches (89% in one study) across the board of coaching approach, and not just psychoanalytically informed coaches, perceive unconscious processes to be relevant to their coaching conversations, and 68% indicate that they occur in the majority of coaching conversations.[156]

With few exceptions, the following features are common to the full range of coaching approaches[157]:

- A systematic process designed to facilitate development (change), whether cognitive, emotional or behavioral
- Intended for a non-clinical population
- An individualized, tailor-made approach
- Aims to encourage coachees to assume charge of their life
- Based on the twin growth areas of awareness and responsibility
- Reliant of the twin skills of listening and questioning
- Involve a collaborative and egalitarian relationship, rather than one based on authority
- Creates a relationship within which the client agrees to be held accountable for the choices she makes
- Designed to access the inner resourcefulness of the client, and built on her wealth of knowledge, experience and intuition

**Directive or non-directive**

The non-directive approach might be summarized as, "the coach manages the process rather than the content of the client's development,"[158] and is "more about asking the right questions than telling people what to do."[159]

In a directive approach, the coach is likely to assume an instructor mode that emphasizes the delivery of guidance, advice, and expert knowledge. This is what is sometimes referred to as *mentoring* as distinct from coaching.

**Development-focused or solution-focused**

Snyder[160] points out how some coaches adopt a pragmatic approach toward their client's problems, while others adopt an exploratory style that seeks to uncover the underlying issues. Solution-focused approaches tend to focus on specific aims and intended outcomes. Personal-development and learning models of coaching seek to address deeper dimensions of personality, based on the premise that doing so enables performance to improve. In fact, this approach advocates addressing all aspects of the person, holding that lasting change cannot be achieved without a fundamental and holistic reorientation.

Development-focused coaching tends to focus on what's holding the person back and is longer-term, while solution-focused coaching tends to focus on what can help to pull the client forward, and is shorter-term.

**Therapeutic versus performance-driven intervention**

The more therapeutic approaches to coaching tend to emphasize the coach-client relationship[161], extending the range and depth of issues that are perceived to be crucial to its success, bringing coaching more in line with the therapeutic relationship. The range or breadth of aspects of the client's life reflects a holistic or systems approach; the depth of issues addressed allows for delving beneath the surface to find less visible or obvious influences that nevertheless may have profound impact on her life patterns and behavior choices.

Is the coaching approach intended to stimulate inner (emotional, psychological, developmental) or outer (cognitive-behavioral, decision-making) change? Is the coaching approach primarily designed to change feelings or actions, personal growth or improved performance?

> Cavanagh (2006, p. 320) makes an important distinction between coaching and therapy based upon complex adaptive systems theory. The purpose of coaching, he argues, is to push the coachee towards the edge of chaos, towards a controlled and managed instability, a condition in which human growth and change is most likely. The role of the coach is to ensure that the coachee does not slip into a state of chaos, in which there is a systems breakdown. This Cavanagh points out is the exact opposite of therapy, which is designed to deal with those who have passed into a state of chaos, and the role of the therapist is to retrieve the client into a state of stability and order. He argues that "therapy seeks to comfort the afflicted. In coaching, however, the coach is often called upon to afflict the comfortable!" In other words, whereas therapy is about restoring stability, coaching is about encouraging a measure of instability.[162]

> The style of coaching we are advocating tends to be humanistic, developmental, and systemic. It tends, therefore, toward being non-directive, developmental, and therapeutic. Yet it is possible to achieve a balance between the extremes of the foregoing categories, maintaining accountability for performance toward goal achievement.

We will be discussing the important distinctions between therapy and coaching next, in a separate chapter of this book. Depending on the orientation of the therapist and of the coach, they may or may not be so different. However, what remains as an ironclad boundary between the two is the nature of the contracting agreement between professional and client.

## The Integrative Coaching Model

The wide variety of approaches to coaching which we have briefly surveyed could seem a bit overwhelming to someone new to coaching. Jonathan Passmore, a British psychologist specializing in executive coaching, has attempted to build an integrated model for executive coaching by bringing together a series of evidence-based approaches. This model uses the concept of coaches working at multiple levels with their clients: behavioral, cognitive, and unconscious. It combines these elements into "streams," which the coach works across seamlessly, moving between streams in the course of their interactions. The Integrative Coaching Model[163] consists of six "streams." The pattern is not fixed and instead responds to the moment to moment changes observed by the coach's developed intuition.

The first stream (developing the coaching partnership) draws on work from the humanistic tradition. This involves positive regard for himself and his coachee; acting openly and honestly, with empathy in his relationship with the coachee; and the coach has the sole objective of meeting the needs of the coachee.

The second stream (maintaining the coaching partnership) draws on both emotional intelligence and aspects from the psychodynamic tradition. Without this initial investment in the relationship, progress on change will be difficult. The work of maintaining the relationship continues through the coaching experience as the coach pays attention to his interactions with the coachee. An effective coach needs to pay attention to three aspects: (1) his own emotions and behaviors; (2) the emotions and behaviors of the coachee; and (3) the coach needs to manage his emotions and adapt his behavioral responses appropriately to maintain both professional detachment while offering personal intimacy. These components make up the building blocks of emotional intelligence.[164,165] Research[166] suggests that those with high emotional intelligence are more likely to be able to form and maintain effective relationships.

The following three streams, where the focus of action and change occurs, deal with behavioral, conscious, and unconscious cognition.

The third stream (behavioral focus) is at the core of all life coaching: behavioral change. The aim is to support behavioral change and to achieve this through deepening the coachee's problem-solving and planning skills.

The fourth stream (conscious cognition) draws upon cognitive–behavioral coaching interventions. The aim of the work in this stream is to deepen the coachee's understanding of the relationship between their thoughts and their behavior, and to challenge those thought patterns when the coachee is holding irrational thoughts that might inhibit successful performance. For example, such irrational thoughts might be harsh judgments about themselves or judgments of their current or future abilities.

The fifth stream (unconscious cognition) focuses on the cognitive processes which are outside of conscious awareness.

The aim of the coach in this stream is to deepen the self awareness of the coachee by bringing into conscious awareness aspects of thought and motivation that inhibit their effective behavioral performance. This stream draws upon the psychodynamic, humanistic, and depth psychology traditions.

A sixth stream surrounds the model. It is the cultural context in which both coach and coachee operate. The coach will consciously hold an awareness of the boundaries and codes which this stream imposes, which may be ethical, legislative, or organizational.

Following is a graphic representation of the Integrative Coaching Model, presented by Passmore.[167]

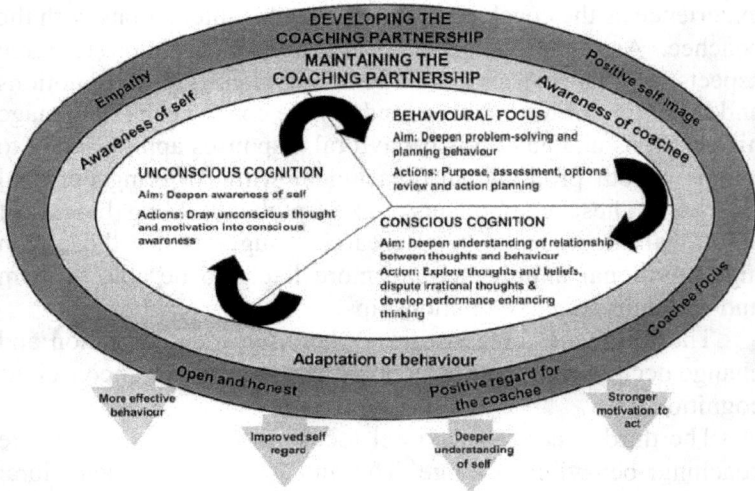

Despite the abundance of theoretical and practical models of coaching, a research meta-analysis[168] indicated there is no significant difference in effectiveness between different coaching techniques, i.e., there is 'outcome equivalence'. Based on this finding, the quality of the coaching relationship as well as the coach and the coachee's role in the process were identified as the most effective common active ingredients for a positive coaching result. A follow up survey study examined and identified the 'helpful' coaches' qualities and behaviors that make for effective coaching; coaches' listening, understanding and encouragement were viewed as the most helpful.[169]

Five key factors have been identified as contributing to a positive and successful coaching relationship[170]:

- Establishing and maintaining a trusting relationship
- Understanding and managing coachees' emotional difficulties is a key factor in the coaching process, since most coachees experience anxiety, sadness and frustration while seeking help from coaches
- Effective two-way communication is considered as an essential ingredient for a harmonious coaching relationship
- Facilitation and help with coachees' learning and development to meet their needs is highlighted a key effectiveness factor
- Clear contract and transparent coaching process is viewed as a vital key factor for establishing a positive relationship, especially at the initial stage of the coaching engagement.

Research has documented that the dynamics of coaching relationships are similar to those in therapy, in particular the working alliance and real relationship between professional and client.[171]

# Chapter Four
# How do Coaching and Psychotherapy Differ?

Some areas of overlap between coaching and psychotherapy/counseling include the similarity in issues brought to the process by clients, i.e., an area of their life that is not working as well as they would like. Both professions are based on an ongoing, confidential, one-to-one relationship between the therapist or coach and his or her client. Both require attention to the relationship itself, clarifying expectations, setting clear professional boundaries, and periodic review of whether the client's needs are being met. Further, many coaches are trained therapists who either have converted their practice from therapy to coaching, or offer both therapy and coaching as alternative services.

The relationship in therapy is more rigidly defined, with dual relationships recognized as problematic, and a sense of protectiveness regarding the client's privacy. The coaching relationship tends to be less formal, with more self-disclosure, active input from the coach, public openness about the relationship, and often more humor.

In general, coaching clients are traditionally high-functioning individuals and relatively free of psychopathology. In fact, coaching is often seen as a method to make high-functioning people perform even better, whereas psychotherapy is principally concerned with treatment of mental disorders. Coaches are viewed as ''facilitators,'' not experts or authorities or healers. The client initiates direction for sessions, i.e., sets the agenda and defines the desired outcomes. Coaches tend to make greater use of technology than do most psychotherapists, including online assessments, e-mail contacts, and teleconferencing-based sessions. Coaching aims to use ''positive diagnosis'' by identifying client strengths, resources, and successes; thus, there is an emphasis on the client's potential for growth and success.[172]

The counselor or therapist, by definition, deals with clients presenting a psychological problem, but also with those wanting personal growth and "wellness". Sometimes a client falls into both categories. The American Counseling Association defines counseling as "The application of mental health, psychological, or human development principles, through cognitive, affective, behavioral or systematic intervention strategies, that address wellness, personal growth, or career development, as well as pathology."[173]

At their core, both are professional relationships and strive for client growth through interpersonal interactions. Both are fundamentally about change and benefit from an understanding of the psychological nature of change.[174] And both benefit by using strengths-based assessments and interventions.[175] Indeed, strengths have already been implicated in successful posttraumatic growth[176], which we will soon discuss.

Coaching is a natural extension of the skill set, objectives, and purpose of psychotherapy. Of course, the focus for the twentieth century was on repairing the negatives of symptoms, traumas, disorders and deficits, aligning the therapy profession with the medical model. Then around the turn of the century a refreshing movement began to gain credibility: positive psychology and positive psychotherapy. Positive psychotherapy contrasts with standard therapeutic interventions for symptoms of mental or emotional dysfunction by *increasing* positive emotion, engagement, character strengths, and meaning rather than directly targeting negative symptoms.[177] A further development in this continuum has taken hold in many parts of the world today: life coaching. Coaching incorporates the added dimension of adult development for *optimal* functioning. Elsewhere we have reviewed several existing conceptualizations of the process of optimal adult development of the ego, or the self: the process of becoming "fully human", represented in the works of Abraham Maslow[178,179], Mark McCaslin[180], Bill Plotkin[181,182], Charles Alexander and colleagues[183], Juan Pascual-Leone[184,185], Jane Loevinger[186], Jack Bauer[187], Susanne Cook-Greuter[188], G. I. Gurdjieff[189] and Oscar Ichazo[190]. For a complete elaboration on this topic, please refer to Hartman & Zimberoff's *Higher Stages of Human Development*.[191] We include here a brief review of some of that research.

In the previous section "The human energy system and energy management", we reflected on a continuum from reparative psychotherapy to life coaching. We are assuming that the coaching client has succeeded in reparative psychotherapy, and is ready to engage the challenges of optimal development, of finding meaning in adversity, and advancing toward life mastery.

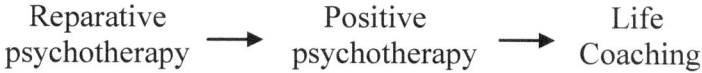

Reparative
psychotherapy  →  Positive
psychotherapy  →  Life
Coaching

Let's consider in more detail the interface between therapy and coaching – the difference between damage repair and optimal growth.

Trauma resolution focuses on building *freedom from* old self-limiting beliefs, areas of arrested development, self-sabotaging behaviors, unconscious dysfunctional motivations, and impulsive or irrational emotional reactivity, what Maslow called the 'fear of one's own greatness'.

Optimal development stimulates one to claim the personal *freedom to* express one's deepest essence, to live spontaneously, to dare to step into one's own greatness, to have the 'arrogance of creativeness' offset by the great humility that comes with transcending one's ego.

Trauma resolution focuses on *object permanence*, i.e., time-stamping experiences to a discreet circumstance rather than a globally generalized re-experience of the original trauma. One of the core aspects of treating PTSD is to route the original traumatic memory through the brain's hippocampus region to time-stamp it, which did not occur during the original trauma.

Optimal development stimulates an individual's sense of *subject permanence*, or the integration of the self-concept, coalescing the 'I' and the 'me'. An enduring 'I' persists through all of the many permutations of 'me' that come and go in my daily experiences, available in the form of a witness consciousness.

Trauma resolution focuses on the "push" from behind by threats or fears to make the changes in one's life necessary to alleviate them, or the unconscious obsession to meet basic needs, such as safety, approval, or self-esteem.

Optimal development motivates with the "pull" from ahead by the promise of fulfillment in becoming one's highest possible self, a transcendent self, of stepping into one's own greatness in order to fulfill one's destiny.

As one progresses from trauma resolution toward higher development, one's perspective on himself, his culture, his environment, and on the world gravitates from an *outside* perspective (the conditioned conventional approach sanctioned by the forces of family, society, culture, science, religion) toward a perspective from the *inside* (autonoetic knowing, intuition, mystical experience).[192] We might call this the "transcendental ego" or "ultraself" as Pascual-Leone does.

> All people have an ordinary adult ego structure, a "phenomenological ego," which is the product of interpersonal interaction, dates from late adolescence, and remains unchanged. Beyond that lies a potential and optional advanced ego, structured solely in terms of internal interactions, the "transcendental ego" or "ultraself." The ultraself is a conscious control center utterly detached from the interpersonal self. This potential will not be realized unless the ordinary adult ego is challenged to make changes in order to overcome obstacles. Only when required will old structures adapt and give rise to new structures.[193]

Therapy for healing trauma
- freedom from . . .
- "object permanence"
- pushed by threat or fear to get basic needs met
- perspective from the outside
- retrospective

coaching for optimal growth
- freedom to . . .
- "subject permanence"
- pulled by the prospect of becoming fully human
- perspective from the inside
- prospective

**Posttraumatic growth, or growth following adversity**

Research on positive changes in the aftermath of adversity has documented the tendency for some people to report growth in five domains: interpersonal relationships, the perception of new possibilities for one's life, personal strength, spirituality, and appreciation for life.[194],[195] Creativity has also been fostered following adversity in highly creative individuals.[196]

Several factors have proven to be instrumental in the development of posttraumatic distress, i.e., disruptions to core beliefs, rumination, and finding meaning.[197][198] These variables have also contributed to the development of posttraumatic growth, the experience of a positive life change as the result of a traumatic experience.[199] Other factors contributing to PTG are deliberate rumination, disclosure, impact on the sense of meaning in one's life, and adaptive coping.

An important distinction to make is that growth following adversity is an increase in *psychological well-being* as opposed to *subjective well-being*.[200]

> Whereas SWB [subjective well-being] reflects affective states and life satisfaction, PWB [psychological well-being] reflects engagement with the existential challenges of life. More specifically, Ryff's (1989; Ryff & Singer, 1996) conceptualization of PWB consists of six aspects; autonomy, environmental mastery, positive relations with others, personal growth, purpose in life, and self-acceptance. Those high on autonomy are self-determining and able to resist social pressures to think and act in certain ways. Those high on environmental mastery have a sense of control and are able to make effective use of opportunities. Those high on personal growth have a feeling of continued development and are open to new experiences. Those high on positive relationships have warm satisfying, trusting relationships with others and are capable of empathy, affection, and intimacy. Those high on purpose in life have goals in life and a sense of directedness and hold beliefs that give life purpose. Those high on self-acceptance possess a positive attitude toward themselves and feel positive about their life.[201]

These questions comprise the Psychological Well-Being – Post-Traumatic Changes Questionnaire, a reliable assessment.

1. I like myself.
2. I have confidence in my opinions.
3. I have a sense of purpose in life.
4. I have strong and close relationships in my life.
5. I feel I am in control of my life.
6. I am open to new experiences that challenge me.
7. I accept who I am, with both my strengths and limitations.
8. I don't worry what other people think of me.
9. My life has meaning.
10. I am a compassionate and giving person.
11. I handle my responsibilities in life well.
12. I am always seeking to learn about myself.
13. I respect myself.
14. I know what is important to me and will stand my ground, even if others disagree.
15. I feel that my life is worthwhile and that I play a valuable role in things.
16. I am grateful to have people in my life who care for me.
17. I am able to cope with what life throws at me.
18. I am hopeful about my future and look forward to new possibilities.

The purpose of the measure is to assess not only the absence of negative functioning but also the presence of positive psychological functioning, i.e., to assess optimal functioning. Posttraumatic growth is thought to arise through the rebuilding of shattered assumptions about the self and the world, such that a positive association is to be expected with self-esteem and optimism. The rebuilding process also involves the person becoming truer to themselves and more appreciative of life, and achieving greater authenticity and gratitude. Adaptive coping (positive reappraisal) refers to attempts to deal with stressful situations by deliberately looking for new ways to positively reframe the situation.

Positive attitude, especially hope and optimistic expectations, and adaptive coping strategies are instrumental in overcoming posttraumatic stress disorder (PTSD) symptoms and creating adaptive outcomes, i.e., posttraumatic growth (PTG) despite co-existing posttraumatic distress.[202] PTG refers to the experience of positive change that can occur in the struggle with highly challenging life crises.[203,204,205] To date, positive changes have been observed from studies on such trauma as medical conditions, disability, personal tragedy, bereavement, or natural disaster.[206]

Resilience is generally defined as one's ability to bounce back after a traumatic experience, returning to one's pretrauma status quo state. PTG, on the other hand, goes beyond adaptation. It is a paradigm shift in one's view of the trauma in order to make meaning out of it, creating significant growth in one's life. Lechner, Antoni, and Carver[207] propose that resilient individuals may fail to regard their traumatic experience as a crisis, hence there is no need for meaning-making because no assumptions have been shattered. This viewpoint is supported through research, with an inverse relationship found between resilience and PTG. The more resilient a person is, the less likely they will exhibit PTG.[208] This bolsters the idea that perceived distress is a necessary precursor to PTG and that resiliency and PTG are two distinct concepts.

Factors that differentiate individuals who thrive following traumatic distress: resilience, hardiness, optimism, and sense of coherence. In particular, Antonovsky[209,210] emphasized that victims who were capable of comprehending, managing to cope, and meaning-making following traumatic experiences were in the best position to thrive. Adaptive coping involves active coping, positive reinterpretation, and seeking social support, whereas maladaptive coping involves denial and behavioral and mental disengagement.[211]

A significant factor in the path from cognitive threat to growth, is the degree to which the person engages in repeated thinking about the event, since repeated thought may lead to an accommodation to the changed reality forced by the traumatic event(s). However, there is an important distinction between deliberate rumination and intrusive rumination.[212] Persons engaging in event-related deliberate rumination intentionally think about the event and its aftermath, whereas persons engaging in event-related intrusive rumination experience thoughts and images about the event that occur automatically and obsessively. Deliberate thinking focuses on understanding the experience, finding meaning, and ultimately producing a revised life narrative and is more conducive to growth than intrusive rumination.[213]

Another factor leading to a greater feeling of well-being is the sense that the struggle with the stressful experience has also led to a change in the sense of meaning in one's life.[214,215] The newfound sense of meaning in life follows the major disruption of people's understanding of the world and their place in it, triggered by the traumatic event, perhaps even a sense that life is meaningless; this fear motivates them to search for meaning in their lives. Survivors may first ruminate about questions regarding the meaning *of* life, but may later shift to ruminating about questions regarding meaning *in* their own lives.[216]

Hardiness reflects existential courage; it is a combination of attitudes that provides the courage and motivation to do the hard, strategic work of turning stressful circumstances from potential disasters into growth opportunities. Hardiness combines the three attitudes of commitment, control, and challenge.[217,218] An individual strong in commitment believes it is important to remain involved with events and people no matter how stressful things become, and to avoid the wasteful effort of withdrawing into alienation and isolation. One who is strong in control wants to continue to have an influence on the outcomes going on around them, no matter how difficult it becomes. An individual strong in challenge sees stress as a normal part of living, and an opportunity to learn, develop, and grow in wisdom.[219]

### When should coaches refer out to a therapist?

Indicators of deeper client issues more appropriate for therapy than coaching include signs of depression, anxiety attacks, alcohol or any addiction, personality disorders, paranoia, a client stuck in a victim role, excessive emotional drama or chaos, not showing up or following through, persistent anger or aggression, suicidal ideation, self-destructive impulses or behaviors, and extreme dependency.

The coach must be clear about the distinction between therapy and coaching, and that distinction needs to be addressed in the initial contract agreement. If the client needs therapeutic intervention before being capable of fully participating in and benefitting from coaching, then it becomes an ethical imperative for the coach to refer the client for therapy. The agreement can certainly include the provision that this client can return to a coaching relationship when the reparative therapy has prepared him properly.

### What should the therapist-turned-coach beware of?

Given that there is a clear and recognized distinction between therapy and coaching, a coach who has been trained as a therapist may encounter difficulty separating the two approaches. Such a coach may, for example, tend to veer into the realm of psychodynamic processing of a coachee's perceived psychopathology, be it anxiety, depression, or rage. Regardless of the coach's training, these are aspects of a client's personality that are not appropriately worked on within the context of a coaching agreement. In coaching the time frame for contacts is not as rigid as in therapy. A coaching session may be half-hour or hour-and-a-half timeblocks, and may be weekly or monthly, and may be brief check-ins by telephone or email, all depending on the contract between the coach and the client.

> Perhaps the biggest obstacle that the therapist-turned-coach needs to be aware of is that coaching is not for every therapist. Coaching models seem best suited to goal-oriented therapists who prefer to enable clients to take responsibility for their own process and outcomes, rather than to "fix" the problem (Steele, 2000).[220]

In short, therapists may need to 'unlearn' therapeutic techniques in which they were previously trained, or at least the propensity to use them, in order to become effective coaches. Unlearn ways of listening for understanding, and learn to listen for recognition of what is meaningful for the client. Unlearn engaging in conversation to get a point across, and learn to engage to invite a client to deeper awareness. Unlearn being curious to seek information, and learn to ask questions that evoke. Unlearn being direct in order to establish a clear request or call to action, and learn to challenge clients to declare chosen actions and decisions.[221]

Even so, a number of studies have pointed out that coaches without fundamental psychology knowledge may not be able to recognize coaching clients' mental health issues and may cause harm to coaching clients.[222, 223,224] All in all, having the training and experience of psychotherapy provides a distinct advantage to effective and ethical coaching.

David Hartman & Diane Zimberoff

# Chapter 5
# Coaching and Hypnosis
# Integrating Hypnotic Strategies into Coaching

As previously stated, the style of coaching we are advocating tends to be humanistic, developmental, systemic, non-directive, and therapeutic. These describe a means toward an end, and the end result must always be achievement of the client's goals.

In this chapter we explore the legitimate place that hypnosis holds in a transpersonal approach to coaching. In particular, we look at the following ways of integrating hypnotic strategies and principles into coaching. Transpersonal coaching incorporates the client's imaginal capacities through engagement of evocative metaphors, images, and creative modalities within the trance state. This liberates free-flow thinking and right-brain processing, yielding access to unconscious processing.

1. Suggestion and suggestive techniques
2. Guided meditation or guided imagery
3. Self-hypnosis
4. Rehearsal
5. Age-progression and age-regression in coaching
6. Dream work

## Coaching and hypnosis

A working paper by the British Psychological Society[225] suggests integrating the theoretical concepts and strategies applied in hypnotherapy and adapting them to the needs of coaching. It also proposes coining the term 'coaching hypnosis' when referring to hypnosis within the coaching arena to distinguish it from therapy.[226]

'Coaching hypnosis' may be referred to as the deliberate use of hypnotic strategies and principles as an adjunct to accepted coaching process.

First it will be instructive to remind the reader that, although hypnosis can be used as a relaxation procedure, hypnosis is not the same thing as relaxation, and relaxation is not even necessarily a part of hypnosis. Hypnosis can be carried out with the individual being physically active, open-eyed, focusing on the external environment and with no suggestions of relaxation.[227,228] Bányai and colleagues have reported on a form of active-alert hypnosis which has proven successful in their psychotherapy practice.[229]

Hypnosis can be very effective within the context of life or executive coaching. For example, hypnosis as well as relaxation techniques are used to help clients relax and lower stress/anxiety, enhance performance, anger management and reduce stress-related symptoms such as tension headaches.[230]

"When appropriate, hypnosis can be used within coaching in a similar way that relaxation and imagery techniques are applied in assisting to reduce performance anxiety and stress."[231]

Hypnosis is a valuable tool in the coaching process, often leading clients to positive coaching breakthroughs.[232]

**Hypnosis and theta brain wave frequency**

Hypnosis and mindfulness generate theta frequency mental activity, the same state as we experience in REM sleep when we are dreaming.

"We know that the neuroscience of mindfulness and hypnosis is parallel, causing changes in brain activation of the same magnitude. Both feature cortical inhibition as revealed by slowed EEG theta waves, and both show higher levels of activity in areas where theta is prominent, such as the frontal cortex and especially the anterior cingulated cortex."[233]

The anterior cingulated cortex (ACC) has been linked to monitoring task performance and the modulation of arousal during cognitively demanding tasks.[234] In other words, this part of the brain decides when to pay attention to the outside world (task-oriented) and when to focus on the internal world (introspection). Both hypnosis and mindfulness meditation states feature higher levels of activity in areas where theta frequency brain waves are prominent, especially the ACC[235,236] and the hippocampus, source of these theta rhythms.[237] These altered states of consciousness, then, offer unique access to the mind's higher-order control of awareness and focused attention. Clearly this phenomenon has important implications for coaching, and provides a convincing argument for the incorporation of the hypnotic state in some coaching activities.

The brain's theta rhythm circuitry is also involved in memory retrieval, survival behavior, navigation including virtual reality tracking, wellbeing, and the integration of emotion and cognition. Hypnosis, which elevates the brain's theta rhythm, assists in memory revivification and the integration of fragmented episodic memories, against a background of anxiety reduction, empowerment and psychic integration.[238]

Another important benefit of the slower frequencies of theta is the brain's opportunity to slow down its task-oriented cognitive processing involving mostly fast-paced beta frequencies. Memory consolidation of one's experience is enhanced when the brain functions at theta frequency, which is increased during hypnosis and occurs in the hippocampus.[239] The brain's theta rhythm circuitry is involved in memory *retrieval* as well as memory *consolidation*. This helps to explain why it is so fortuitous to access and correct old beliefs, release old perseverating memories, and construct new paradigms within the theta-rich hypnotic trance state.

## Access to "procedural" implicit memory

Regarding memory retrieval, the state of hypnosis provides ready access to layers of mental processing that normal everyday consciousness does not. The information that was encoded in memory before language gave names to things is an example. In hypnosis, people frequently "remember" the experience of early childhood or even their birth. Since these source experiences and their embedding in memory were accomplished in an altered state (e.g., trauma or right brain dominated early childhood), they are "state-dependent" and accessing them is accomplished more easily by returning to the source state. We will explore ways in which retrieving core beliefs that are deeply embedded in such memories can be highly appropriate in coaching.

## Neural networks

Hypnosis affects the brain, as well as the thoughts and beliefs processed by the brain, through the process of *neuroplasticity* and *neurogenesis*. The brain is constantly adapting to new information and new circumstances, e.g., modifying patterns of connection between different parts of the brain and reorganizing neural pathways and functions (neuroplasticity), as well as developing new neurons (neurogenesis).

An example of modifying connections is using hypnosis to develop new neural pathways within the *corpus callosum*, the major highway between the two hemispheres of the brain, which is reduced through the effects of stress and trauma.[240] Another example is found with patients who suffer chronic fatigue syndrome, which has the symptoms of persistent fatigue and a decrease in cortical gray matter volume. After successful hypnotherapy which addresses faulty thoughts and beliefs about the condition, patients not only feel better but also show a significant increase in gray matter volume localized in the lateral prefrontal cortex (an area related to the speed of cognitive processing).[241]

> These are examples of how the state of hypnosis actually enhances the brain's *neuroplasticity* and *neurogenesis*. Many of the functions of effective coaching are amplified through interventions that incorporate hypnosis, mindfulness, and theta-rich mental processing.

Several discreet resting-state networks have been identified. At the highest hierarchical level, there are two opposing systems in charge of intrinsic and extrinsic processing, respectively. They are the *default mode network*, a network of regions that show high metabolic activity and blood flow at rest but which deactivate during goal-directed cognition; and an *attention system* which attends to a specific task at hand but deactivates during periods of rest.[242]

| *default mode network* | *attention system* |
|---|---|
| self-referential processes | goal-directed cognition |
| reconstructing the past or | sensory-related tasks |
| simulating the future (such as | motor- related tasks |
| fantasy, inner rehearsal, | language- related tasks |
| and daydreaming) | attention-related tasks |
| imagination | |

Regions included in the attention system network show a synchronized activity in absence of any specific cognitive activity, that is, at rest, while they are known to be engaged during sensory-, motor-, language- or attention-related tasks. As for the default mode network, it includes brain areas associated with multiple high-order functions that are generally stimulus-independent and thus self-referential processes. These can be related to organizing memory such as reconstructing the past; simulating the future such as fantasy, inner rehearsal and daydreaming; and imagination such as free association, stream of consciousness, and taking other people's perspective.

Insight into the default mode network shows us what advantages the hypnotic trance state or a mindfulness meditative state offers one to facilitate just these activities related to past, future, and other people's perspective. In short, the default network is responsible for self-projection—mentally transporting oneself into alternate times, locations, or perspectives—as manifested in episodic memory, navigation, prospection (i.e., anticipating future events), and theory of mind (taking another's perspective).[243] Self-projection into alternative pasts and futures actually offers vitally important applications to our work in coaching. One is that understanding the default mode network can help to identify and explain, and potentially access, preconscious and unconscious mental activity such as moodiness, prejudice, irrational fears, or uncontrollable anger. Another is that some default mode functions may be brought under conscious control and direction, potentially through hypnotic trance states. Thus, a coach may be able to guide a client to reframe a past failure as a valuable learning experience, to gain a new perspective on the perplexing behavior patterns of a colleague, or to vividly envision a desired future that is outside the client's current capacity to imagine.

This is the case because mindfulness meditative states or hypnotic trance states allow access to both the focused attention of executive function and the relaxed openness of default mode *at the same time*.

One part of the brain is particularly important as an interface switch between executive function and default mode function, and is referred to as the salience network.[244] It is primarily the anterior cingulate cortex (ACC) which has been linked to monitoring task performance and the modulation of arousal during cognitively demanding tasks.[245] In other words, this part of the brain decides when to pay attention to the outside world (task-oriented) and when to focus on the internal world (introspection). Both hypnosis and mindfulness meditation states feature higher levels of activity in areas where theta frequency brain waves are prominent, especially the ACC[246,247] and the hippocampus, source of these theta rhythms.[248] These altered states of consciousness, then, offer unique access to the mind's higher-order control of awareness and focused attention. And it is precisely these functions that are so crucial for coaching success.

Most states of consciousness carry an anticorrelation between 'rest' and goal-directed behavior, between self- and external-awareness networks, between openness and focused attention; the more awareness is focused on internal processing (introspection, or self-awareness), the less it is available for attention to sensory input (external awareness) and goal-directed focus, and vice-versa. The hypnotic trance state is an exception; parts of the brain that are normally activated with an opposite on/off switch can be dissociated from each other to allow both to activate at the same time. Under hypnosis, the anterior cingulated cortex (ACC) is activated which narrows attention. But, unlike in the waking state of narrowed attention, the posterior attentional system which stimulates vigilance is *de*activated during hypnosis.[249] Thus hypnosis creates a state of dual effect: relaxation yet responsiveness. The conscious mind is calmed, enabling access to the unconscious mind. Maldonado and Spiegel[250] define this as 'trance logic' – a way of reasoning that does not follow the rules of 'normal' logical processes. Through this mechanism, an individual may have experiences and interpret them in ways that are not in accordance with the person's conscious rational belief system.[251]

In a similar dual effect, meditation has been shown through fMRI and EEG studies to activate both the sympathetic and parasympathetic nervous systems simultaneously, creating a calm state with enhanced alertness.[252] There is, in addition, increased activity in the reward pathway, particularly the hippocampus and the amygdala during meditation,[253] with increased levels of dopamine,[254] as there is under hypnosis.

However, there is a marked neural difference between hypnosis and meditation. In hypnosis, a decrease occurs in functional connectivity across the hemispheres, measured by EEG gamma band coherence,[255] while in meditation there is an increase in this coherence between and within hemispheres.[256] EEG coherence normally means more of the brain is being used, with an associated improvement in quality of attention. In the case of hypnosis, the decrease in coherence indicates a dissociation, or decoupling, of attention to more than one thing rather than a decrease in mental processing. This dissociation allows one to attend to apparently incongruous thoughts; for example a person can experience being a child of seven in age regression and at the same time experience being a healthy adult available to nurture that child.

## Integrating hypnotic strategies and principles in coaching

### Suggestion and suggestive techniques

Suggestion and suggestive techniques, while traditionally associated with hypnosis and Neurolinguistic Programming (NLP), can be usefully applied by the coach in almost any format of interaction with a client. In other words, hypnosis is not a requirement for suggestive influence. Professionals with training in hypnosis and NLP will be familiar with the importance of properly structuring suggestions. We will review the technology of constructing effective suggestions, following the elaboration provided by Steckler[257] and Yapko[258].

1. **Keep the suggestions simple and easy to follow**. Complicated and sequential suggestions engage the client's conscious mind, rendering unconscious process less available for access.
2. **Use your client's language**. The coach's words and language may not have the same meaning for the client. Further, the coach can miss important cues in the role of the client's unconscious as expressed by the words the client selects. This is especially true for idiosyncratic usage. "Pissed off" is not the same as "angry". Yapko cites an example of a client who used the word "telegraph" in what seemed an unusual way. In trancework with her, it evolved

that her father had received a "telegraph" to go to war, never
to return, a memory lost to consciousness by the client, but
one which affected her trust in male relationships into the
present.

3. **Have the client define everything**. What constitutes a
"phobia" or "depression" for the coach may not be the same
experience for the client. If the client defines what he or she
means, both connotation and denotation are alike for coach
and client.

4. **Use the present tense and a positive structure**. It is
important to phrase suggestions in terms of what a person
can do, rather than in terms of what they can't do. "I am now
an organized person . . ." rather than "I want to get more
organized." Also, link the present to the future: "As you are
doing this, you can also begin to do that."

5. **Encourage and compliment the client**. A respectful regard
for the client is crucial. Encouragement, rather than attack or
critical reproach, allows the client to move to a position of
acknowledging personal strengths and resources, allowing
for self-generated change.

6. **Determine ownership of the problem**. It is difficult to
facilitate change in people who see themselves as "victims,"
who are "other-blamers." Helping people to discover that
they can control their reactions to life events is in fact one
component of the hypnotic experience, helping to establish
an acceptance set for subsequent owning of responsibility.

7. **Determine the best modality for the trance experience**.
People experience the world through their senses, and
Bandler and Grinder[259] have hypothesized that people utilize
a preferred sensory mode in their thinking, and further that
they express this preference in their language. Some people
think in pictures, while others favor the auditory modality,
remembering conversations with clarity or recalling their
inner dialogue during particular experiences. Still others
express themselves in kinesthetic terms, remembering
primarily the feeling components of experience. While each
person processes experience in terms of all modes,
identifying a client's preferred mode can allow the coach to
couch communications in the words of the favored system,

increasing the likelihood of facilitating client change because of the improved communicative rapport.

8. **Keep the client only as informed as is necessary to succeed**. An advantage of hypnotic communication is its ability to make contact with the client's affective rather than cognitive domain. While this may present an ethical dilemma at one level, Yapko advocates handling this on a sensitive case-by-case basis. He notes that telling a client about using a confusional technique to disrupt a maladaptive thinking pattern will effectively destroy the gain of the technique. Dealing with affect inevitably has a greater impact than dealing strictly with intellect: "I know (cognitive) I shouldn't feel this way, but I do (affective)."

9. **Give your clients the time they need**. Everyone responds according to their own pace, and it is crucial that the coach remain patient and flexible with the coaching agenda.

10. **Get permission before touching your client**. Always ask before intruding on personal space. Respect the client's physical integrity. Touching without permission may also reorient the client outwardly, diminishing the inward focus of trance.

11. **Establish anticipation signals**. To avoid startling clients, always say, "In a moment I am going to . . ." Anticipation signals foster trust in the hypnotic communication.

12. **Use a voice and demeanor consistent with your intent**. It is a therapeutic contradiction to urge relaxation in a stressed, tense voice. Further, soothing tones discourage intellectual analysis, thus further facilitating trance.

13. **Chain suggestions structurally**. Hypnosis can be utilized to build a link between what the client is doing and what he will do. This can be done with "and" or "but" ("You are sitting here and beginning to feel relaxed"); or with implied causatives such as "as," "while," and "during" ("As you notice yourself breathing more comfortably, you can begin to remember your birthday"). However, the strongest link is the causative predicate, suggesting a current behavior will cause a future one ("Thinking of your birthday will make you remember other holidays").

14. **Be general specifically**. Avoid the use of detail in suggestions. The more specifics one provides, the more likelihood of the client's contradicting the suggestion.
15. **If desirable, substitute other terms for hypnosis**. Some clients are afraid of "hypnosis" but welcome the idea of progressive relaxation, focused imagery, and other hypnotic techniques by other names. Possible additional alternative labels are deep relaxation, controlled relaxation, visual imagery, guided imagery, guided fantasy, guided meditation, or mental imagery. However, as Yapko points out, if a focused state of attention is narrowed to suggestions offered, and influence then occurs, hypnosis is present.

Use of suggestion is not manipulation. Manipulation involves the intention to get someone to do what you want. Coaches use suggestions for the sole purpose to meet the client's agenda, not their own. It is goal-directed communication when a coach says, "This will help you improve your performance – I can already see the difference!" while offering the client feedback about improvements to his public speaking.

An individual is more receptive to suggestion in a hypnotic trance state than when she is in her everyday cognitive mindset. One way of capitalizing on this receptivity is to use *presuppositions*. You get the client thinking that something desired has already happened, is now happening, or is inevitably about to happen. A coach might communicate the presumption that something is about to happen, establishing a positive expectancy for the client by saying, "Allow a time to come to you when you felt confident, and when you are there raise a finger to let me know" (presupposing that an appropriate time will come). Another example of using this technique is to present a choice, either of which accomplishes the task, such as "Would you like to discuss this today or during our next meeting?" or "'I wonder where you'll start to implement your clear priorities first. Will it be at work with your clients or at home with your family?"

We communicate the presumption that something is happening when we say, "That's right, now continue relaxing" or "Allow this sense of purpose to spread throughout your body." And the coach suggests to the client that something has already happened when she says, "Notice the calm excitement you are feeling as you breathe deeply and recall that experience."[260]

These suggestions presented as presumptions are important in the wording of guided imagery or hypnotic facilitation. A coach trained in the use of hypnosis is very familiar with phrases such as, "Now you are beginning to feel confident and well-organized as you sit at your desk and review the day's top priorities," or "Beaming confidence, you recognize the respect that each colleague sitting at the conference table has for you." Notice how important it is to use descriptive language to bring the client's awareness directly into the situation being imagined, and to link the task with strong emotions.

Repetition is a powerful reinforcement for any suggestion. The coach's suggestions will be more successfully received and acted on when the main message is repeated several times throughout the coaching session, thereby repeatedly directing attention to the intended goal or idea.

State suggestions as a positive, gearing them toward a desirable goal rather than away from an unwanted one. Rather than "Don't let others' judgments about you stop you from following your plan", the client will respond better to "You love the sense of freedom that comes with absolute confidence in the rightness of your plan."

## Guided meditation or guided imagery

Guided meditation or guided imagery is very helpful for mindfulness, relaxation, and de-stressing. Coaches can bring guided meditation or guided imagery to the attention of their clients to help them enhance performance as well as to reduce stress.[261] The technique is also sometimes referred to as *imagery rescripting*.

A variation of these techniques is *anticipated memory* – visualizing future thoughts that help to frame hopes and dreams and make them become real.[262]

A specific example of guided imagery is presented by Alcid M. Pelletier[263] as an excellent technique for establishing goals. Although she writes the instructions for use by a psychotherapist, the technique is equally useful in a coaching context.

## A Creative Thematic Apperception Test

The psychotherapist lightly relaxes the patient by verbal suggestions while the patient faces a painting on the counseling room wall. A plethora of paintings which are colorful with an abundance of recognizable and natural detail may be used.

Once the patient is relaxed the therapist gives instructions much as one does in administering the Thematic Apperception Test. "Please look *into* the painting *there.* Let your *imagination* become *very active* until *your* activity seems *very real* and enjoyable. *Be aware* of *every* detail of your *activity there.* (Italicized words are emphasized for deeper suggestion).

The patients have been instructed in ideomotor responses to signal the therapist whenever they are actively involved in the scene. "Now please tell me *your* story. How did it *begin?* Then tell me *exactly* what's *happening* in your *present* involvement. Then, follow *the story* on to its conclusion so *we will know* the *ending.* As soon as the story ends you will remain relaxed and everything will be like it was before the involvement in the story." Bring the patient out of trance.

Stories dealing with past or present events in the client's life are helpful in diagnostic procedures and indicating the need for the use of psychodynamic work or possibly referral for psychotherapy. Stories which are future oriented can be helpful to assist in determining previously unacknowledged possibilities and the establishment of goals.

## Self-hypnosis

Research findings show that many individuals with little or no previous experience with hypnosis expect that hypnosis induced by a professional would be experienced as involuntary, but that self-hypnosis would be experienced as voluntary.[264] Therefore a coach who intends to utilize hypnosis in the engagement may want to introduce the client to self-hypnosis to empower a sense of self-efficacy and to diminish possible resistance.

Self-hypnosis is an accessible and effective means of following through on many of the practices a coach may facilitate for the client, either during the coaching session or in between sessions.

- Practicing/rehearsing skills.
- Facilitating learning.
- Regaining control.
- Maintaining motivation.
- Accessing resources.
- Goal attainment

**Rehearsal**

Hypnosis is an excellent vehicle for exploring an individual's internal imagery and conclusions that may be unconsciously influencing a client's everyday choices in life. If the coaching focus at any one point in time is on interpersonal relations, dealing with conflict, approaching competition, or one's personal level of organization, it may be very useful for the client to understand what unconscious influences are at work. Of course it is important to access positive, supportive associations as well as negative, inhibiting ones.

An example of incorporating hypnosis into coaching is using it to neutralize negative elements and promote adaptive responses in rehearsing competitive situations.[265] Understanding the source of a current performance deficit is half the process of resolving it, and in the hypnotic trance state, in age regression, the coach can effectively assist the client to access early conflicted experiences and to release the original debilitating beliefs and conclusions (e.g., "Other people are unreliable", or "Conflict is scary and I always lose", or "Competition is threatening because it means the winner is boastful and the loser is humiliated").

Then the second half of the healing process is to find early experiences of success in the area of current focus, and to amplify and anchor viscerally that experience. Perhaps the client remembers a time in grade school when she won a spelling bee and was jubilant while remaining gracious with the other children competing in the spelling bee. We then want to anchor that resource state with a word or phrase, a color, an image, or a somatic experience. It becomes a powerful inner resource which can be called on in a rehearsal of the problematic situation in the client's present day life. In hypnosis, we would implement a mental rehearsal technique in which the client recalls herself in a current day challenging situation that felt like failure, and give the suggestion to let the memory fade. Now, in a moment, she would go back into that same situation, and first find compassion for herself in light of the early conditioning she has now uncovered. Next, still in that same situation, she is encouraged to use her anchors to recall her resource, her inner strength, and her new perspective, to feel the strong presence of her compassionate, secure self.

Because our visceral experience is so much a part of the pattern of behavior we want to change, we can use hypnotic and self-hypnotic techniques to de-condition the automatic reactions and replace them with more adaptive responses. Perhaps the client's heart tends to race and her hands begin to perspire when confronted with a conflictual situation at work. We can again use the anchors already established to calm that automatic sympathetic nervous system response in a rehearsal of an actual work-related conflict. The client can experience in mental rehearsal a calmness, an alert but open perspective, a composed heart and dry confident hands.

If it is useful with a given coachee, the TV technique[266] can be used to review troublesome situations "with the emotional volume turned down," enabling a client to more objectively identify elements of success as well as obstacles to problem-solve.

Finally, Hornyak[267] suggests utilizing hypnosis to develop protective buffers for highly challenging environments. It is a fact that there will be people and situations that we would prefer to avoid but cannot. It may help the client in such a situation first to use the anchors she rehearsed to establish confidence, calm, and to not take it personally. Then it may be helpful for her to create a metaphor such as learning to "take your sail out of their wind" or participating in the situation with the dispassionate perspective of the TV technique. The client may want to visualize the daunting boss or co-worker as an immature child, or as a particular animal to accurately remember who one is dealing with and to neutralize their impact. The client could create an imaginary structure such as a protective bubble, or suits of armor to protect herself and reduce the absorption of toxicity from others.

Rehearsing recently taught coping strategies; rehearsing benefits and gains in order to increase motivation; and identifying problems that may arise and managing them in advance are all applications that rely on age-progression.

## Age-progression and age-regression

We have discussed a number of ways that age-progression and age-regression can be adapted to fit a coaching approach. For example, age regression was utilized to go back to times in the client's life when they expressed their signature strength with confidence, or dealt successfully with transitions. Likewise, age-progression is an integral part of an *anticipated memory* conjured in a guided imagery process, or of the various processes we have elaborated in work with the potential future self.

As well, time projection imagery can be included to demonstrate to the coachee that they can tolerate current difficult or challenging situations, moving the perspective ahead to a time when he/she can imagine the current challenge has been mastered or resolved.[268]

In an age-progression experience, the client can imagine and explore an image of his/her future. What do they want to do or feel? What is it like? What is needed to get there? Are there any anticipated difficulties? From the vantage point of this imagined future, the client may find it easier to recognize clear goals and what success looks like and feels like. What resources and personal skills are needed? What coping mechanisms will need to be developed in order to make this vision a reality?

When looking back from this potential future, what would make you think, "I handled this well." Within the non-defensive state of hypnosis, a client may be more open and receptive to feedback from that future self than she is from her current day self.

Age regression applications include accessing resources that 'once were' and building on them; accessing desired resources or skills that already exist in another area and 'transfer' them to the immediate need; and review previous performance in order to build on positives and develop what's missing. For example, a client may have been out of the work force for a period of time and lack confidence in her ability to do well in a job interview. The coach could take her back to a time that she did very well in a similar situation, and she could anchor the feeling of confidence.

### Dream work

An important part of the coach's role is to help clients with their journeys into self-awareness. Manfred F. R. Kets de Vries[269] suggests that, to help coachees with their journey into their own interior, coaches can also pay attention to their clients' dreams. Clients' dreams can offer useful clues about their main out-of-awareness preoccupations and concerns, their internal struggles and challenges. Making sense of dreams can be a very powerful problem-solving and inspirational tool as well – the theta-rich dream environment is highly creative and free of many of the mental limitations that dominate our everyday thought processing.[270]

Dreaming is a state in which we can access our inner selves, find inner resources to discover new solutions not available in our waking state. Dreams can open our perspective on what is possible, beyond our self-limiting everyday beliefs and behaviors.

Of course, revealing their dreams to a coach may be personally challenging for many clients, fearing that their dreams may unmask parts of themselves unknown even to themselves. That may be a degree of vulnerability too far so some. Even the idea of incorporating dream work into life coaching may strike some as outlandish, "new age", or a waste of time. Working with their coach over time will hopefully nurture a growing sense of trust in the coach and his expertise (even if it includes dream work).

Clearly, the dream belongs to the dreamer, and the interpretation of it also belongs to the dreamer. A qualified coach will not offer interpretations of dreams, but only listen intently, ask probing questions, and suggest possible correlations to other material the client has brought to the coaching relationship.

Coaches may ask the client to reflect on their dream imagery to encourage uncovering the meaning of the dream. For example, what emotions did they experience? Were they scared, angry, embarrassed, joyful, jealous, disgusted? Did they still have those feelings when awake? How comfortable were they with those feelings? Can they identify any recurring thoughts associated with their dreams? If so, in what other situations have they had them?

An even more kinesthetic method for helping the client to realize the messages in the dream is to ask the client to have a dialogue with certain dream elements, those that hold the most fascination or disturbance. "John, now that you've identified how intensely you react to the policeman in your dream, I suggest that you *become* the policeman for a moment and speak to John, the dreamer. Tell him why you have acted the way you did in this dream, why you said what you did, and what message are you in the dream to deliver to John?" Then allow John to address the policeman dream element, and for a dialogue to develop between the two. You can proceed to do a similar process with other symbols in the dream that are particularly engrossing to the client.

> I do realize that this kind of work is not for every executive coach. Dreams are full of discontinuities, ambiguities, and inconsistencies that can be downright bizarre, necessitating nonconformist thinking, acceptance of ambiguity, and flexibility of thought. In dreams, content and organization are illogical; the conventional notions of time, place, and person do not apply; and natural laws are disobeyed. Sense-making becomes a kind of detective work, for both client and coach. . . .
>
> Executive coaches should view dreams as stories or puzzles that clients must solve to be free.[271]

Another way of working with dreams is to approximate them in the waking state so that the coach is available to participate directly. The **waking dream technique**[272], developed by Dr. Paul Schenk, is similar to a daydream, and consists of having the client go into a relaxed state, after which the coach might advise the subject that he or she relax and go within even more deeply. The subject might then find himself or herself beginning to imagine being someone in a movie: a person whose story will contain experiences that will be timely, useful, and constructive for them in their own life. A client who has unfettered access to her imagination and who is willing to share it with the coach without inhibition will produce valuable dreamlike imagery and storylines.

Coaches are well-advised to incorporate their clients' imaginal capacities through engagement of evocative metaphors, images, and creative modalities within the trance state or otherwise. Encourage free-flow thinking, right-brain thinking, intuition, and storytelling. These are ways of accessing the client's unconscious processing that often uncover aspects of herself and her interpersonal relationships that are known neither to her nor to others.

# Chapter 6
# The Heart-Centered Approach to Coaching
# Transpersonal Coaching

As previously stated, the style of coaching we are advocating tends to be humanistic, developmental, systemic, non-directive, and therapeutic. These describe a means toward an end, and the end result must always be achievement of the client's goals.

In this chapter we explore the following:
1. Applying a developmental approach to coaching
2. Applying Psychodynamic Approaches to Coaching
3. Applying Gestalt Approaches to Coaching
4. Applying positive psychology to coaching
5. Applying transpersonal psychology to coaching

**Applying a developmental approach to coaching**

Developmental theorists (Erik Erikson, Jane Loevinger) believe that we move to new stages of development irrespective of our success at mastering the cognitive/affective challenges of

---

We know through the work of Loevinger, Torbert and others that at any one point in time, an individual is about 50% anchored in their current dominant stage, about 25% lagging in the previous stage there are moving beyond, and about 25% focused in anticipation on the stage they are moving toward.

Effective coaching recognizes the coach's facilitation is aimed at accelerating the client's advancement to their next stage. To do so masterfully requires a coach to assist the client to assess their lagging edge and use remedial means to nurture it to "catch up", and their leading edge in order to identify the direction that will lead them to greater productivity and fulfillment. And hypnosis is valuable in both of these functions. People often find that they are more willing and able to nondefensively recognize their lagging edges in the altered state than in their left-brain everyday state. Likewise, people often discover through the altered state a more open and less self-limiting vision of future possibilities.

the current stage. When we move to another stage, yet have not mastered the challenges of the stage from which we just moved, then we carry the burdens of this previous stage to the new stage, making it more difficult to meet the new challenges associated with the new stage.

### Applying psychodynamic approaches to coaching

Typically, a coach is hired to assist an individual or group to meet tangible goals: increase productivity, increase teamwork or decrease interpersonal conflict. Most of the coach's interventions are just as tangible and practical as the stated goal. The coachee may need to learn something (e.g., diplomacy or how to better organize his time), or he may need to refine an underdeveloped skill (e.g., delegating effectively or appropriate self-care). But sometimes in the course of working through such practical agenda items, it becomes clear that invisible forces are at work that must be discovered and dealt with, perhaps underlying anxiety about self-worth or fear of failure, a deep mistrust of the opposite gender or a fear of success.

One way of conceptualizing this, and presenting it to a coachee, is what Ekman[273] refers to as "importing a script" from the past into the current situation. That is, an earlier significant event (e.g., being rejected by a significant female or being socially punished for a personal success) is seen as similar to the current situation such that reactions to the earlier event (e.g., rage or fear) may occur in the current situation. The individual being coached may not see any connection between early life events and current day problematic behavior, and sometimes the coach may need to educate his client about the pervasive but invisible influence that early experience has on today's life choices.

Westin[274] summarized the research evidence that has accumulated for five key postulates of psychodynamic theory and the legacy of Sigmund Freud. Those propositions can be summarized as follows:

1. Much of human mental life, including thoughts, emotions, and motives, are unconscious and can produce behavior in people that is inexplicable to them.

2.  Conscious and unconscious thoughts and feelings operate simultaneously and can be in conflict with each other in ways that require compromised resolutions.
3.  Stable patterns of personality and social behavior are formed in childhood and can significantly impact the types and effectiveness of social relationships in adult life.
4.  Stable internal mental representations of the human self are formed gradually in childhood and adolescence and guide both social relationships and how individuals may become psychologically symptomatic.
5.  Personality development involves learning how to regulate emotions, thoughts, and social relationships and moves from an immature, dependent state in childhood to a mature and independent state in adulthood.

In light of the previous discussion of the difference between coaching and psychotherapy, how do we discern what is appropriate territory in the client's inner world within the context of coaching?

Kilberg[275] suggests a number of situations in which unconscious material may well prove useful to consider, and therefore employing a psychodynamic approach in coaching may be called for. In general, he advises it when the coach sees patterns of dysfunctional behavior in individuals, groups, or whole organizations on which more conventional change methodologies fail to have any truly constructive effect. Also, he identifies fifteen situations that indicate the appropriate use of a psychodynamic approach, which we summarize below:

1.  when strong emotional states are encountered in clients or when they face major transitions in their personal or organizational lives.
2.  when performance problems for individual executives, their groups, or their organizations have contributing circumstances that are out of the awareness of the people involved.
3.  when nuclear families and families of origin of executives create major areas of unrevealed tension and conflict.

4. when the client may be sufficiently curious and psychologically well-developed that he or she has a natural ability and willingness to explore these dimensions of human experience.

He also has a clear warning for the coach who makes the choice to incorporate this deeper level of working with the coachee. "Diagnostic acumen and professional judgment are central to determining whether the shadow realm of psychodynamics should be entered." [276] There may be times when the therapist-turned-coach may feel more at home with the psychodynamic realm, with family of origin issues, intrapsychic conflict, defenses, and transference issues in the coaching relationship, than with the tangible task of improving the coachee's productivity. The overriding question to stay focused on is, "How can I best serve my client's greatest needs within the parameters of our initial contract agreement?"

There are clearly times when referral to a therapist is in order. If a coach finds herself working far more on client reactions to early trauma events, relationship issues outside of work, defensive and emotional reactions unrelated to the goals of the coaching agreement, or unconscious conflicts that seem only tangentially related to the confines of the coaching agreement, then the activity has probably slid into therapy. A referral would be in order, or a serious change in coaching strategy.

## Applying Gestalt approaches to coaching

Coaching is generally oriented to identifying the client's goals to pursue, and working with the resistance patterns that interfere with his ability to realize those goals. The Gestalt approach to coaching conceptualizes resistance as an adaptive and positive force that serves a protective function for the client; resistance must not be "overcome", but rather brought into awareness and worked through in a way that enables the client to recognize its constructive function and to re-channel its energy as a support in the current situation. We apply the same process as with "shadows" when we encounter resistance in the context of psychotherapy.

With the same spirit of openness to experimenting, Gestalt coaching offers a safe arena where clients can take personal risks exploring their vulnerability and strong emotions, knowing that failure is a valuable pathway to learning and growth. This approach exemplifies the Gestalt Paradoxical Theory of Change: change does not occur by trying to be what one isn't, but by fully embracing who one is.[277]

> The Paradoxical Theory of Change is the overarching Gestalt theoretic perspective for the coaching encounter. A fundamental intervention in Gestalt coaching is to sharply focus attention on what already exists for the client in the present, with the paradoxical result of initiating a profound experiential shift towards something new. This perspective acknowledges that the client is in fact his or her own "expert," and that the coach's strongest function is to provide a supportive presence, to be a collaborative partner, and to serve as the witness to the client's work and learning.[278]

Attending to one's own sensations, emotions, and thoughts (including interpretations and judgments) is a good practice for staying present in the moment. When we truly experience what usually goes unnoticed, new perspectives begin to arise.

The Gestalt *Cycle of Experience* was first developed at the Gestalt Institute of Cleveland, and our discussion of it flows from Dorothy Siminovitch's work. Awareness of the this cycle provides the coach skilled in a Gestalt approach with a way of identifying more precisely where processes become "stuck," i.e., where the client's resistance has stepped in attempting to create safety. The Cycle of Experience also helps the coach to create interventions that will heighten clients' awareness of their behavioral pattern, helping clients to recognize for themselves the habitual locations and patterns of their becoming stuck. Where in the process of problem solving does the client tend to become anxious, to struggle with setting new boundaries, to withdraw, or to extend their activation when it is time to rest?

The Cycle of Experience is a vehicle for examining both internal and external reality, and emphasizes the need to come full circle in order to fully integrate experience. A person (or group) approaches a new experience from a state of rest sensing multiple processes occurring internally and externally:

- A sensation claims the attention
- Awareness develops inducing anxiety/excitement, mobilizing energy for action
- Action leads to contact with a new boundary, creating the conditions for change

- Successful contact is followed by withdrawal and assimilation
- Closure re-structures experience and a return to a state of rest

# CYCLE of EXPERIENCE

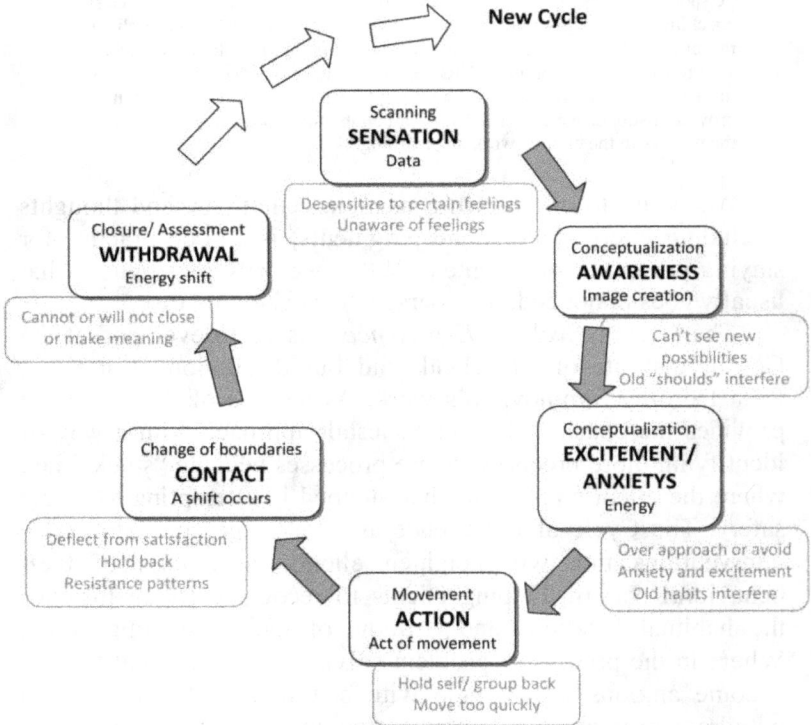

New Cycle

Scanning
**SENSATION**
Data

Desensitize to certain feelings
Unaware of feelings

Closure/ Assessment
**WITHDRAWAL**
Energy shift

Conceptualization
**AWARENESS**
Image creation

Cannot or will not close
or make meaning

Can't see new
possibilities
Old "shoulds" interfere

Change of boundaries
**CONTACT**
A shift occurs

Conceptualization
**EXCITEMENT/
ANXIETYS**
Energy

Deflect from satisfaction
Hold back
Resistance patterns

Over approach or avoid
Anxiety and excitement
Old habits interfere

Movement
**ACTION**
Act of movement

Hold self/ group back
Move too quickly

Another valuable Gestalt technique that a coach may choose to employ is *role reversal*. The coach might suggest that the client take the place of whoever is problematic in his reaching his goal. If the client feels insecure with a supervisor, for example, the coach could ask him to "become" that supervisor and talk directly to the client. It will bring to the surface what the client's fears and assumptions are, regardless of whether they are projections onto the supervisor or accurate observations of the other's perspective. Role reversal is also a good exercise for stretching the client's willingness to loosen her attachment to identifying with the persona she is comfortable with.

## Applying positive psychology to coaching

A basic principle from the field of positive psychology is *appreciative inquiry*, which advocates focusing first on what works in an individual, group or organization.[279,280,281] Only after identifying the areas that are working well, the strengths and successes, would the coach begin to explore the problems and what is not working adequately. Clients feel energized by the elaboration of what is going well in their work and in their life. This allows them to feel more hopeful about the future and less defensive about changes that are required.

We have already discussed the usefulness of the *VIA Signature Strengths Inventory*[282] in assisting individuals to clarify their personal virtues and character strengths. Using it may be an excellent way to begin a coaching engagement and to focus awareness on the client's strengths when he/she is likely preoccupied with deficiencies.

The state of mind that seems to be most conducive to being productive and feeling happy tends to concentrate and engage one's attention in goal-oriented activities of a particular nature. "Flow" is the term Mihalyi Csikszentmihalyi[283] coined to name this state which is described as:

1. feeling like effortless action;
2. involving goals that demand specific responses and where clear, relevant feedback is available;
3. involving activities that require high levels of skill and concentration;
4. generating a "paradox of control," meaning the feeling of being nearly out of control—yet feeling exhilarated at the completion of the task because one was able to maintain control over one's movements or the environment; and
5. losing self-consciousness—while untroubled by worry about what others may think.

Sandra Foster and Paul Lloyd, each a psychologist and coach, recommend using the Experience Sampling Method (ESM) to help clients gain an awareness of how they spend their time.[284] Time management is a fertile area for coaching intervention. The ESM is a self-report method that prompts the respondent in random real time to notice what activity she is engaging in and to categorize her feeling about it. The individual asks herself these questions: (1) At this moment, what are you doing and with whom (or are you alone)? (2) How satisfied are you right now? Rate your answer on a scale from 0 to 10 where 0 is "not at all satisfied—I'm bored" to 10, which means "I am completely satisfied with what I am doing." (3) How much skill is required for this activity? (4) Describe your level of motivation as you engage in this activity. (5) How challenged do you feel by this activity? Rate your answer on a scale from 0, "This activity presents no challenge whatsoever. I could do it on autopilot," to 10, "This activity presents an extremely demanding challenge for me." And (6) How much are you concentrating on what you are doing at this moment? The answer is rated from 0, "I am completely distracted and paying no attention at all," to 10, "I am completely absorbed and engaged in what I am doing and cannot think about anything else." They have found that activities tend to fall into three categories:

1. Productive Activities—for example, working to earn a living, studying, talking over a problem with others at work, daydreaming about projects while at work, volunteering, and commuting;

2. Leisure—falling into two types: passive and active. Passive leisure is defined as watching TV or videos, hanging out, resting, or being idle (surfing the Net, online chat that has become routine). Active leisure is expressed in hobbies, playing sports, playing music, attending live theater or music concerts (more mental engagement than watching on TV or videos), socializing, and cooking.

3. Maintenance activities— grooming, shopping, cleaning, waiting in line, and "mindless" food preparation (to be contrasted with cooking with a high level of engagement).

This exercise can result in powerful insights for an individual who wants to maximize their productivity and/or the experience of flow in their life. This is especially true when time management or procrastination are identified in the initial contract agreement as behavior patterns to address in the coaching engagement.

**Applying transpersonal psychology to coaching**

By transpersonal psychology we mean integrative/ holistic psychology, a psychology of transformation and transcendence beyond ego. Maslow's "transcending self-actualization" foresaw the development of the exploration of the transpersonal realm within psychology, advancing beyond humanistic psychology. Lajoie and Shapiro[285] identified a number of major themes in the field of transpersonal psychology: states of consciousness, higher or ultimate potential, beyond the ego or personal self, transcendence, and the spiritual. Levin[286] suggests that the major characteristics of the transpersonal discipline comprise the search for goals and the meaning of life, the strengthening of inner personal resources, and the belief in transcendental abilities for self-growth.

These themes are all legitimately addressed in a coaching environment in which the client finds it useful to explore, and which has explicitly identified them in the initial agreement. Transpersonal coaching allows a domain spacious enough to incorporate spirituality, community and collective experiences of humankind, influences on beliefs and behavior that reside deep in one's unconscious, the meaningfulness of life, and our energetic interactions with the natural world.

While many might assume that the task of the coach is to reduce, remove or resolve the client's experience of conflict, great creativity is found when one tolerates the "tension of the opposites" (Carl Jung's term). The transpersonal approach in coaching emphasizes the value of the questions even more than the value of the answers, because asking the *right* questions is so vitally important to getting the *best* answers.

# References

Adams, G. R., & Fitch, S. A. (1982). Ego stage and identity status development: A cross-sequential analysis. *Journal of Personality and Social Psychology, 43*, 574-583.

Ai, A. L., Tice, T. N., Whitsett, D. D., Ishisaka, T., & Chim, M. (Jan 2007). Posttraumatic symptoms and growth of Kosovar war refugees: The influence of hope and cognitive coping. *The Journal of Positive Psychology, 2*(1), 55–65.

Alexander, C. N., Davies, J. L., Dixon, C. A., Dillbeck, M. C., Oetzel, R. M., Druker, S. M., Muehlman, J. M., & Orme-Johnson, D. W. (1990). Growth of higher stages of consciousness: Maharishi's Vedic psychology of human development. In C. N. Alexander & E. J. Langer (Eds.), *Higher Stages of Human Development: Perspectives on Adult Growth*, 286-341. New York: Oxford University Press.

Allcorn, S. (2006). Psychoanalytically informed executive coaching. In D. R. Stober & A. M. Grant (Eds.), *Evidence Based Coaching Handbook*, 129-152. New York: Wiley.

American Counseling Association. (1997). Definition of professional counseling. http://www.counseling.org.

American Psychological Association. (February 2005). Guidelines for Education and Training at the Doctoral and Postdoctoral Level in Consulting Psychology/Organizational Consulting Psychology. Society of Consulting Psychology.

American Society of Clinical Hypnosis. (2009). *Code of Conduct.*

Antonovsky, A. (1987). The salutogenic perspective: Toward a new view of health and illness. *Advances, 4*, 47–55.

Antonovsky, A. (1993). The implications of salutogenesis: An outsider's view. In A. P. Turnbull, J. M. Patterson, S. K. Behr, D. L. Murphy, J. G. Marquis, & M. Blue-Banning (Eds.), *Cognitive Coping, Families, and Disability*, 111–122. Baltimore, MD: Paul H. Brookes Publishing.

Armatas, A. (Sept 2009). Coaching hypnosis: Integrating hypnotic strategies and principles in coaching. *International Coaching Psychology Review*, 4(2), 174-183.

Armatas, A. (2011). Suggestive techniques in coaching. *Coaching: An International Journal of Theory, Research and Practice*, 4(1), 32-41

Asalone, S. "What Do You Do With A Strengths Assessment?" December 27, 2010. Available at http://positivepsychologynews.com/news/scott-asalone/2010122715665

Aspinwall, L. G., & Staudinger, U. M. (Eds). (2003). *A Psychology of Human Strengths: Fundamental Questions and Future Directions for a Positive Psychology*. Washington DC: American Psychological Association.

Astin, J. A., Anton-Culver, H., Schwartz, C. E., Shapiro, D. H., McQuade, J., Breuer, A., Taylor, T. H., Lee, H., & Kurosaki, T. (1999). Sense of control and adjustment to breast cancer: The importance of balancing control coping styles. *Behavioral Medicine,* 25(3), 101-109.

Auerbach, J. E. (2006). Cognitive coaching. In D. R. Stober & A. M. Grant (Eds.), *Evidence Based Coaching Handbook*, 103-128. New York: Wiley.

Bachkirova, T. (Autumn 2004). Dealing with issues of the self-concept and self-improvement strategies in coaching and mentoring. *International Journal of Evidence Based Coaching and Mentoring*, 2(2), 29-40.

Bandler, R., & Grinder, J. (1975). *The Structure of Magic I*. Palo Alto, CA: Science and Behavior Books.

Bányai, E., Zseni, A., & Tury, F. T. (1997). Active-alert hypnosis in psychotherapy. In J. Rhue, S. Lynn, & I. Kirsch (Eds.), *Handbook of Clinical Hypnosis*. Washington, DC: American Psychological Association.

Barabasz, A. F., & Barabasz, M. (2008). Hypnosis and the brain. In M. R. Nash, & A. J. Barnier (Eds.), *The Oxford Handbook of Hypnosis: Theory, Research, and Practice*, 337-364. Oxford, UK: Oxford University Press.

Bauer, J. J. (2008). How the ego quiets as it grows: Ego development, growth stories, and eudaimonic personality development. In H. A. Wayment & J. J. Bauer (Eds.), *Transcending Self-interest: Psychological Explorations of the Quiet Ego*, 199-210. Decade of Behavior. Washington, DC: American Psychological Association.

Bauer, J. J., & McAdams, D. P. (2004). Growth goals, maturity, and well-being. *Developmental Psychology*, 40(1), 114-127.

Beisser, A. R. (1970). The paradoxical theory of change. J. Fagan and I. Shepherd (Eds.), *Gestalt Therapy Now*. Palo Alto: Science and Behavior Books.

Berg, I. K., & Szabo, P. (2005). *Brief Coaching for Lasting Solutions*. New York: W. W. Norton & Company.

Berger, J. (2002). The use of hypnosis and relaxation therapy in professional and life skills coaching. *Australian Journal of Clinical Hypnotherapy and Hypnosis*, 23(2), 81-88.

Berger, J. G. (2006). Adult development theory and executive coaching practice. In D. R. Stober, & A. M. Grant (Eds.), *Evidence Based Coaching Handbook*, 77-102. New York: Wiley.

Berglas, S. (2002). The very real dangers of executive coaching. *Harvard Business Review, 80*, 87–92.

Bion, W. R. (1963). *Elements of Psychoanalysis*. London: Heinemann.

Biswas-Diener, R. (2009). Personal coaching as a positive intervention. *Journal of Clinical Psychology: In Session*, 65(5), 544-553.

Bohart, A. (Apr 1983). *Detachment: A variable common to many psychotherapies?* Paper presented at the 63rd annual convention of the Western Psychological Association, San Francisco.

Boud, D., Cohen, R., & Walker, D. (1994). *Using Experience for Learning*. Buckingham, England: SRHE and Open University Press.

Bowlby, J. (1969). *Attachment and Loss, Vol. 1. Attachment*. New York: Basic Books.

British Psychological Society. (2001). *The Nature of Hypnosis: Report Prepared by a Working Party at the Request of the Professional Affairs Board*. Leicester, UK.

Brown, D. P., & Fromm, E. (1986). *Hypnotherapy and Hypnoanalysis*. Hillsdale, NJ: Lawrence Erlbaum Associates.

Buckley, A. (Summer 2007). The mental health boundary in relationship to coaching and other activities. *International*

*Journal of Evidence Based Coaching and Mentoring*, Vol. Special Issue, 17-23.

Buckner, R. L., & Carroll, D. C. (2007). Self-projection and the brain. *Trends in Cognitive Sciences*, 11, 49–57.

Burns, D. D. (1989). *The Feeling Good Handbook: Using the New Mood Therapy in Everyday Life*. New York: William Morrow.

Calhoun, L. G., & Tedeschi, R. G. (1999). *Facilitating Posttraumatic Growth: A Clinical Guide*. Mahwah, NJ: Erlbaum.

Calhoun, L. G., Cann, A., & Tedeschi, R. G. (2010). The posttraumatic growth model: Socio-cultural considerations. In T. Weiss & R. Berger (Eds.), *Posttraumatic Growth and Culturally Competent Practice: Lessons Learned from Around the Globe*, 1–14. Hoboken, NJ: Wiley.

Cann, A., Calhoun, L. G., Tedeschi, R. T., Triplett, K. N., Vishnevsky, T., & Lindstrom, C. M. (Mar 2011). Assessing posttraumatic cognitive activity: The Event Related Rumination Inventory. *Anxiety, Stress, & Coping*, 24(2), 137-156.

Capafons, A. (2004). Waking hypnosis for waking people: Why in Valencia? *Contemporary Hypnosis, 21*(3), 136–145.

Carlberg, G. (1997). Laughter opens the door: Turning points in child psychotherapy. *Journal of Child Psychotherapy, 23,* 331–349.

Caruso, D., & Salovey, P. (2004). *The Emotionally Intelligent Manager: How to Develop and Use the Four Key Emotional Skills of Leadership*. San Francisco: Jossey-Bass.

Carver, C., Scheier, M., & Weintraub, J. (1989). Assessing coping strategies: A theoretically based approach. *Journal of Personality and Social Psychology*, 56, 267–283.

Caspi, J. (Oct 2005). Coaching and social work: Challenges and concerns. *Social Work,* 50(4), 359-362.

Cavanagh, M. (2006). Coaching from a systemic perspective: A complex adaptive conversation. In D. R. Stober, & A. M. Grant (Eds.), *Evidence Based Coaching Handbook*, 313-354. New York: Wiley.

Childre, D., & McCraty, R. (2001). Psychophysiological correlates of spiritual experience. *Biofeedback*, 29(4), 13-17.

Cohen, K., & Collens, P. (Nov 2012). The impact of trauma work on trauma workers: A metasynthesis on vicarious trauma and vicarious posttraumatic growth. *Psychological Trauma: Theory, Research, Practice, and Policy*, 5(6), 570-580.

Cook-Greuter, S. R. (Oct 2000). Mature ego development: A gateway to ego transcendence? *Journal of Adult Development*, 7(4), 227-240.

Cooperrider, D. (1995). Introduction to appreciative inquiry. *Organizational Development* (5th ed.). New York: Prentice Hall.

Cooperrider, D., Sorensen, P., Whitney, D., & Yaeger, T. (Eds.). (1999). *Appreciative Inquiry: Rethinking Human Organization Toward a Positive Theory of Change.* Champaign, IL: Stipes.

Corbetta, M., & Shulman, G. L. (2002). Control of goal-directed and stimulus-driven attention in the brain. *National Review of Neuroscience*, 3, 201–215.

Costa, P. T., Jr., & McCrae, R. R. (1994). Stability and change in personality from adolescence through adulthood. In C. F. Halverson, G. A. Kohnstamm, & R. P. Martin (Eds.), *The Developing Structure of Temperament and Personality from Infancy to Adulthood*, 139-150. Hillsdale, NJ: Erlbaum.

Cox, E. (2006). An adult learning approach to coaching. In D. R. Stober, & A. M. Grant (Eds.), *Evidence Based Coaching Handbook*, 193-218. New York: Wiley.

Cox, E., & Ledgerwood, G. (2003). 'The New Profession'. *International Journal of Evidence Based Coaching and Mentoring*, 1(1).

Critchley, H. D., Wiens, S., Rotshtein, P., et al. (2004). Neural systems supporting interoceptive awareness. *Natural Neurosciences*, 7, 189-95.

Crumbaugh, J. C., & Maholick, L. T. (1964). An experimental study in existentialism: The psychometric approach to Frankl's concept of noogenic neurosis. *Journal of Clinical Psychology*, 20(2), 200-207.

Csikszentmihalyi, M. (1990). *Flow: The Psychology of Optimal Experience*. New York: Harper & Row.

Dahlsgaard, K., Peterson, C., & Seligman, M. P. E. (2005). Shared virtue: The convergence of valued human strengths across culture and history. *Review of General Psychology*, *9*(3), 203-213.

de Haan, E. (2008). *Relational Coaching: Journeys Towards Mastering One-To-One Learning*. Chichester: John Wiley & Sons.

de Haan, E. (2008a). I doubt therefore I coach: Critical moments in coaching practice. *Consulting Psychology Journal: Practice And Research*, *60*(1), 91-105.

de Haan, E. (2008b). I struggle and emerge: Critical moments of experienced coaches. *Consulting Psychology Journal: Practice And Research*, *60*(1), 106-131.

de Haan, E., & Nieß, C. (2012). Critical moments in a coaching case study: Illustration of a process research model. *Consulting Psychology Journal: Practice and Research*, *64*(3), 198-224.

de Haan, E., Culpin, V., & Curd, J. (2011). Executive coaching in practice: What determines helpfulness for clients of coaching. *Personnel Review, 40*(1), 24–44.

de Lange, F. P., Koers, A., Kalkman, J. S., Bleijenberg, G., Hagoort, P., van der Meer, J. W. M., et al. (2008). Increases in prefrontal cortical volume following cognitive behavioral therapy in patients with chronic fatigue syndrome. *Brain*, 13(8), 2172-2180.

Deikman, A. J. (1982). *The Observing Self*. Boston: Beacon Press.

Dutton, J. (2003). *Energize Your Workplace: How to Create and Sustain High-Quality Connections at Work*. San Francisco, CA: Jossey-Bass.

Eidelson, R. J., D'Alessio, G. R., & Eidelson, J. I. (2003). The impact of September 11 on psychologists. *Professional Psychology: Research and Practice*, 34, 144–150.

Ekman, P. (2003). *Emotions Revealed: Recognizing Faces and Feelings to Improve Communication and Emotional Life*. New York: Holt.

Ellis, A. (1979). The practice of rational-emotive therapy. In A. Ellis & J. Whiteley (Eds.), *Theoretical and Empirical Foundations of Rational-Emotive Therapy*. Monterey, CA: Brooks/Cole.

Ellis, D. (2006). *Life Coaching: A Manual for Helping Professionals*. Carmarthen, Wales: Crown House Publishing Ltd.

Engler, J. (1983). Vicissitudes of the self according to psychoanalysis and Buddhism: A spectrum model of object relations development. *Psychoanalysis and Contemporary Thought*, 6(1), 29-72.

Epstein, M. (1988). The deconstruction of the self: Ego and "egolessness" in Buddhist insight meditation. *Journal of Transpersonal Psychology*, 20(1), 61-69.

Erikson, E. H. (1963). *Childhood and Society*, 2nd ed. New York: W. W. Norton & Co. (Original work published 1950).

Erikson, E. H. (1969). *Gandhi's Truth*. New York: W. W. Norton & Co.

Erikson, E. H. (1994). *Childhood and Society*. New York: Norton. (Original work published 1950).

Feltz, D. L., Chase, M. A., Moritz, S. E., & Sullivan, P. J. (Dec 1999). A conceptual model of coaching efficacy: Preliminary investigation and instrument development. *Journal of Educational Psychology*, 91(4), 765-776.

Findeisen, B. R.. (Autumn 1995). Primal Process and Higher Personality. *Primal Renaissance: The Journal of Primal Psychology*, 1(2), 2-21. Available online at http://www.primalspirit.com/pr1_2findeisen_higherpersonali ty.html.

Forgeard, M. J. C. (Aug 2013). Perceiving benefits after adversity: The relationship between self-reported posttraumatic growth and creativity. *Psychology of Aesthetics, Creativity, and the Arts*, 7(3), 245-264.

Foster, S. L., & Lloyd, P. J. (2007). Positive psychology principles applied to consulting psychology at the individual and group level. *Consulting Psychology Journal: Practice and Research*, 59(1), 30-40.

Frankl, V. E. (1960). Beyond self-actualization and self-expression. *Journal of Existential Psychiatry*, 1, 5-20.

Frankl, V. E. (1967). *Psychotherapy and Existentialism: Selected Papers on Logotherapy*. New York: Simon & Schuster.

Fredrickson, B. (2001). The role of positive emotions in positive psychology: The broaden-and-build theory of positive emotions. *American Psychologist, 56*, 218-226.

Freud, S. (1953). *The Standard Edition of the Complete Psychological Works of Sigmund Freud* (J. Strachey, Ed. and Trans.). London: Hogarth Press.

Gardner, H. (1999a). *Intelligence Reframed: Multiple Intelligences for the 21st Century*. New York: Basic Books.

Gardner, H. (1999b). *The Disciplined Mind*. New York: Simon & Schuster.

Gould, D. (1987). Your role as a youth sports coach. In V. Seefeldt (Ed.), *Handbook for Youth Sport Coaches*, 17-32. Reston, VA: American Alliance for Health, Physical Education, Recreation, and Dance.

Grant, A. M. (2003) The impact of life coaching on goal attainment, metacognition and mental health. *Social Behavior and Personality*, 31(3), 253-264.

Grant, A. M. (2006). An integrative goal-focused approach to executive coaching. In D. R. Stober & A. M. Grant (Eds.), *Evidence Based Coaching Handbook*, 153-192. New York: Wiley.

Grant, A. M., & Stober, D. (2006) Introduction. In D. R. Stober & A. M. Grant (Eds.), *Evidence Based Coaching Handbook*. New York: Wiley.

Grassie, W. (May 2007). The new sciences of religion. *The Global Spiral, Metanexus*, 8(2). Available online at http://www.metanexus.net/magazine/tabid/68/id/9925/Defau lt.aspx.

Gray, D. E. (2006). Executive coaching: Toward a dynamic alliance of psychotherapy and transformative learning processes. *Management Learning*, 37, 475–497.

Greenberg, L. S. (2002). Integrating an emotion-focused approach to treatment into psychotherapy integration. *Journal of Psychotherapy Integration*, 12(2), 154-189.

Greenberg, M., & Maymin, S. (Aug 14, 2008). Manage your team's energy, not just the work. *Positive Psychology News Daily*. Retrieved from http://positivepsychologynews.com/news/margaret-greenberg-and-senia-maymin/20080814932.

Grove, D. J., & Panzer, B. I. (1989). *Resolving Traumatic Memories: Metaphors and Symbols in Psychotherapy*. New York: Irvington Pub.

Gurdjieff, G. I. (1963). *Meetings with Remarkable Men*. New York: Penguin Putnam.

Hamachek, D. E. (1978). *Encounters with the Self* (2nd Ed.). New York: Holt Rinehart and Winston.

Harding, C. (Autumn 2006). Using the Multiple Intelligences as a learning intervention: A model for coaching and mentoring. *International Journal of Evidence Based Coaching and Mentoring*, 4(2), 19-42.

Hargrove, R. (2000). *Masterful Coaching Fieldbook*. San Francisco: Jossey-Bass/Pfeiffer.

Hart, V., Blattner, J., & Leipsic, S. (2001). Coaching versus therapy: A perspective. *Consulting Psychology Journal: Practice And Research*, *53*(4), 229-237.

Harter, S. (1999). *The Construction of the Self: A Developmental Perspective*. London: The Guilford Press.

Hartman, D., & Zimberoff, D. (2008). Higher Stages of Human Development. *Journal of Heart-Centered Therapies*, 11(2), 3-95.

Harvey, J. (July 2, 2014). Knowing Why Coaching Works: It Matters. *Library of Professional Coaching*. Retrieved from http://libraryofprofessionalcoaching.com/research/evidence-based/knowing-why-coaching-works-it-matters/.

Hatfield, E., & Cacioppo, J. T. (1994). *Emotional Contagion: Studies in Emotion and Social Interaction*. New York and Cambridge: Cambridge University Press.

Hawkins, P. & Smith, N. (2007). *Coaching, Mentoring, and Organisational Consultancy: Supervision and Development*. New York: Open University Press.

Hawkins, P., & Smith, N. (2010). Transformational coaching. In E. Cox, T. Bachkirova & D. Clutterbuck (Eds.), *The Complete Handbook of Coaching*, 231–244. London: Sage.

Helson, R., & Roberts, B. W. (1994). Ego development and personality change in adulthood. *Journal of Personality and Social Psychology*, 66, 911-920.

Hick, S. F. (2008). Cultivating therapeutic relationships: The role of mindfulness. In S. F. Hick & T. Bien (Eds.), *Mindfulness and the Therapeutic Relationship*, 3-33. New York: Guilford Press.

Hill, N. (2008). *The Law of Success: The Master Wealth-Builder's Complete and Original Lesson Plan for Achieving*

*Your Dreams*. New York: Tarcher. (originally published in 1928)

Hill, P. C., and Pragament, K. I. (2003). Advances in the conceptualization and measurement of religion and spirituality. *American Psychologist*, 58(1), 64-74.

Hoffman, E. (1996). *Future Visions: The Unpublished Papers of Abraham Maslow*. Thousand Oaks, CA: Sage.

Holmes, T. H., & Rahe, R. H. (1967). The Social Readjustment Rating Scale. *Journal of Psychosomatic Research*, 11(2), 213–218.

Hornyak, L. M. (2004) Competition: How Hypnosis Can Help Women to Hold Their Own in the Workplace. *American Journal of Clinical Hypnosis*, 47(1), 13-20,

Hufford, D. J. (Sept 2008). Visionary Spiritual Experiences and Cognitive Aspects of Spiritual Transformation. *The Global Spiral*, volume 9, issue 5. Available online at http://www.metanexus.net/magazine/tabid/68/id/10610/Defa ult.aspx.

Hy, L. X., & Loevinger, J. (1996). *Measuring Ego Development (2nd ed)*. Mahwah, NJ: Lawrence Erlbaum.

Ichazo, O. (1982). *Interviews with Oscar Ichazo*. Arica Press.

Ives, Y. (Aug 2008). What is 'Coaching'? An Exploration of Conflicting Paradigms. *International Journal of Evidence Based Coaching and Mentoring*, 6(2), 100-113.

James, W. (1981). *The Principles of Psychology* (2 Vols). Cambridge, MA: Harvard University Press. (Original work published 1890).

Janoff-Bulman, R. (1992). *Shattered Assumptions: Towards a New Psychology of Trauma*. New York: The Free Press.

Janoff-Bulman, R. (2006). Schema-change perspectives on posttraumatic growth. In L. G. Calhoun & R. G. Tedeschi (Eds.), *Handbook of Posttraumatic Growth: Research and Practice*, 81–99. Mahwah, NJ: Erlbaum.

Jencke, W. (Oct 7, 2008). Balance and health: How do positive emotions lead to good health? *Positive Psychology News Daily*. Retrieved online from http://positivepsychologynews.com/news/wayne-jencke/200810071062.

Joseph, S., & Linley, A. (2005). Positive adjustment to threatening events: An organismic valuing theory of growth through adversity. *Review of General Psychology*, 9, 262–280.

Joseph, S., Maltby, J., Wood, A. M., Stockton, H., Hun, N., & Regel, S. (2012). The Psychological Well-Being – Post-Traumatic Changes Questionnaire (PWB-PTCQ): Reliability and validity. *Psychological Trauma: Theory, Research, Practice, and Policy*, 4(4), 420–428.

Jung, C. G. (1961). The stages of life. In *Modern Man in Search of a Soul*. London: Routledge & Kegan Paul. (Originally published in 1931).

Jung, C. G. (1973). *Memories, Dreams, Reflections*. New York: Pantheon Books.

Kabat-Zinn, J. (1990). *Full Catastrophe Living: Using the Wisdom of Your Body and Mind to Face Stress*. New York: Delacorte.

Kauffman, C. (2006). Positive psychology: The science at the heart of coaching. In D. R. Stober & A. M. Grant (Eds.), *Evidence Based Coaching Handbook*, 219-254. New York: Wiley.

Kauffman, C., & Scoular, A. (2004). Towards a positive psychology of executive coaching. In P.A. Linley & S. Joseph (Eds.), *Positive Psychology in Practice*, 287–302. Hoboken, NJ: Wiley.

Kemp, T. (2006). An adventure-based framework for coaching. In D. R. Stober, & A. M. Grant (Eds.), *Evidence Based Coaching Handbook*, 277-312. New York: Wiley.

Kets de Vries, M. R. (2014). Dream journeys: A new territory for executive coaching. *Consulting Psychology Journal: Practice And Research*, 66(2), 77-92.

Kilburg, R. R. (2004). When shadows fall: Using psychodynamic approaches in executive coaching. *Consulting Psychology Journal: Practice And Research*, 56(4), 246-268.

Kitchener, K. S., King, P. M., Davison, M. L., Parker, C. A., & Wood, P. K. (1984). A longitudinal study of moral and ego development in young adults. *Journal of Youth and Adolescence*, 13, 197-211.

Knowles, M. (2005). *The Adult Learner*. Burlington, MA: Elsevier.

Kobasa, S. C. (1979). Stressful life events, personality, and health: An inquiry into hardiness. *Journal of Personality and Social Psychology*, 37, 1–11.

Kolb, D. A. (1984) *Experiential Learning: Experience as the Source of Knowledge and Development*. Englewood Cliffs, NJ: Prentice-Hall.

Koltko-Rivera, M. E. (2006). Rediscovering the later version of Maslow's hierarchy of needs: Self-transcendence and opportunities for theory, research, and unification. *Review of General Psychology*, 10(4), 302-317.

Krishnamurti, J. (1964). The problem of freedom. In D. Rajagopal (Ed.), *Krishnamurti: Think on These Things*, 9-17. New York: HarperCollins.

Lajoie, D. H., & Shapiro, S. I. (1992). Definitions of transpersonal psychology: The first twenty-three years. *Journal of Transpersonal Psychology*, 24(1), 79–94.

Langer, E. (1989). *Mindfulness*. New York: Addison-Wesley.

Lechner, S., Antoni, M. H., & Carver, C. S. (2006). Curvilinear associations between benefit finding and psychosocial adjustment to breast cancer. *Journal of Consulting and Clinical Psychology*, 74, 828–840.

LeDoux, J. E. (1996). *The Emotional Brain: The Mysterious Underpinnings of Emotional Life*. New York: Simon & Schuster.

Levin, D. (2009). *Walking Betwixt the Worlds: The Alchemy of the Soul*. Tel Aviv: Notza Vakeset publishers. Printed in Hebrew.

Levine, S. Z., Laufer, A., Stein, E., Hamama-Raz, Y., & Solomon, Z. (2009). Examining the relationship between resilience and posttraumatic growth. *Journal of Traumatic Stress*, 22, 282–286.

Levinson, D. J. (May 1977). The mid-life transition: A period in adult psychosocial development. *Psychiatry: Journal for the Study of Interpersonal Processes*, 40(2), 99-112.

Levinson, D. J. (1990). A theory of life structure development in adulthood. In C. N. Alexander & E. J. Langer (Eds.), *Higher Stages of Human Development: Perspectives on Adult Growth*, 35-53. New York: Oxford University Press.

Levinson, H. (1996). Executive coaching. *Consulting Psychology Journal: Practice and Research*, 48, 118–123.

Linley, A. P. (2008). *Average to A+: Realising Strengths in Yourself and Others*. Coventry, UK: CAPP.

Linley, P. A., & Joseph, S. (2004). Positive change following trauma and adversity: A review. *Journal of Traumatic Stress*, 17, 11–21.

Loehr, J., & Schwartz, T. (2003). *The Power of Full Engagement: Managing Energy, Not Time, Is the Key to High Performance and Personal Renewal*. New York: Free Press.

Loevinger, J. (1976). *Ego Development: Conceptions and Theories*. San Francisco: Jossey-Bass.

Lyubomirsky, S. (2007). *The How of Happiness. A Scientific Approach to Getting the Life You Want*. New York: Penguin Press.

Maddi, S. R. (July 2006). Hardiness: The courage to grow from stresses. *The Journal of Positive Psychology*, 1(3), 160–168.

Maddi, S. R., & Kobasa, S. C. (1984). *The Hardy Executive: Health Under Stress*. Homewood, IL: Dow Jones-Irwin.

Maldonado, J. R., & Spiegel, D. (1998). Trauma, dissociation, and hypnotisability. In J. D. Bremner & C. R. Marmar (Eds.), *Trauma, Memory and Dissociation*. Washington DC: American Psychiatric Press.

Martin, J. R. (1997). Mindfulness: A proposed common factor. *Journal of Psychotherapy Integration*, 7, 291-312.

Martin, J. R. (2002). The common factor of mindfulness – an expanding discourse: Comment on Horowitz (2002). *Journal of Psychotherapy Integration*, 12(2), 139-142.

Maslow, A. H. (1943). A theory of human motivation. *Psychological Review*, 50, 370-396.

Maslow, A.H. (1954). *Motivation and Personality*. New York: Harper.

Maslow, A. H. (1968). *Toward a Psychology of Being*. New York: Van Nostrand Reinhold.

Maslow, A. H. (1971). *The Farther Reaches of Human Nature*. New York: Penguin Books.

Maslow, A. H. (1971b). Theory Z. In A. H. Maslow, *The Farther Reaches of Human Nature*, 270-286. New York: Penguin Books.

Maslow, A. H. (1979). *The Journals of A. H. Maslow* (R. J. Lowry, Ed.; Vols. 1-2). Monterey, CA: Brooks/Cole.

Maslow, A. H. (1994). *Religions, Values, and Peak Experiences.* New York: Penguin Books (originally published in 1970).

Maslow, A. H. (1996). Critique of self-actualization theory. In E. Hoffman (Ed.), *Future Visions: The Unpublished Papers of Abraham Maslow*, 26-32. Thousand Oaks, CA: Sage.

Masters, R. A. (2000). Compassionate wrath: Transpersonal approaches to anger. *Journal of Transpersonal Psychology*, 32(1), 31-51.

Mayerson, N. M. (2013). Signature strengths: Validating the construct. Presentation to International Positive Psychology Association, Los Angeles, CA, 82-83.

McCaslin, M. L. (June 2008). The nature of transpersonal leadership: Building potential relationships. *Integral Leadership Review*, 8(3). Available online at http://www.integralleadershipreview.com/archives/2008-06/2008-06-article-mccaslin.html.

McConkey, K. M. (1986). Opinions about hypnosis and self-hypnosis before and after hypnotic testing. *International Journal of Clinical and Experimental Hypnosis*, 34, 311–319.

McCraty, R., Tiller, W., & Atkinson, M. (1996). Cardiac coherence: A new, noninvasive measure of autonomic nervous system order. *Alternative Therapies in Health and Medicine*, 2(1), 52-65.

Metcalf, M. (Mar 2008). 'Level 5 Leadership': Leadership that transforms organizations and creates sustainable results. *Integral Leadership Review*, 8(2). Available online at: http://integralleadershipreview.com/5136-feature-article-level-5-leadership-leadership-that-transforms-organizations-and-creates-sustainable-results/

Metzner, R. (1980). Ten classical metaphors of self-transformation. *Journal of Transpersonal Psychology*, 12(1), 47-62.

Metzner, R. (Aug 1997). The re-unification of the sacred and the natural. *Eleusis*, No. 8. Available online at http://www.rmetzner-greenearth.org/reunify.html.

Naughton, J. (2002). The coaching boom: Is it the long-awaited alternative to the medical model? *Psychotherapy Networker*, 42, 1–10.

Neenan, M., & Dryden, W. (2013). *Life Coaching: A Cognitive-Behavioural Approach*. New York: Routledge.

Nelson, E., & Hogan, R. (Mar 2009). Coaching on the dark side. *International Coaching Psychology Review*, 4(1), 7-19.

Noam, G. G. (1998). Solving the ego development-mental health riddle. In P. M. Westenberg, A. Blasi, & L. D. Cohn (Eds.), *Personality Development*, 271-295. Mahwah, NJ: Lawrence Erlbaum Associates.

Oakley, D. A., & Halligan, P. W. (2010). Psychophysiological foundations of hypnosis and suggestion. In S. J. Lynn, J. W. Rhue, & I. Kirsch (Eds.), *Handbook of Clinical Hypnosis*, 79–118.Washington, DC: American Psychological Association.

O'Neill, M. B. (2007). *Executive Coaching with Backbone and Heart—A Systems Approach to Engaging Leaders with their Challenges*. San Francisco: Jossey-Bass.

Palmer, S. (Nov 2008). The judicious use of hypnosis in coaching and coaching psychology practice. *International Coaching Psychology Review*, 3(3), 253-262.

Palmer, S., & Dryden, W. (1995). *Counselling for Stress Problems*. London: Sage.

Park, C. L. (2010). Making sense of the meaning literature: An integrative review of meaning making and its effect on adjustment to stressful events. *Psychological Bulletin*, 136, 257–301.

Pascual-Leone, J. (1990). Reflections on life-span intelligence, consciousness, and ego development. In C. N. Alexander & E. J. Langer (Eds.), *Higher Stages of Human Development: Perspectives on Adult Growth*, 258-285. New York: Oxford University Press.

Pascual-Leone, J. (2000). Mental attention, consciousness, and the progressive emergence of wisdom. *Journal of Adult Development*, 7(4), 241-254.

Passmore, J. (2007). An integrative model for executive coaching. *Consulting Psychology Journal: Practice and Research*, 59(1), 68–78.

Passmore, J., & Marianetti, O. (2007). The role of mindfulness in coaching. *The Coaching Psychologist*, 3(3), 131–137.

Pelletier, A. M. (1979). Three uses of guided imagery in hypnosis. *American Journal of Clinical Hypnosis*, 22(1), 32-36.

Peterson, C., Park, N., Pole, N., D'Andrea, W., & Seligman, M. E. P. (2008). Strengths of character and post-traumatic growth. *Journal of Traumatic Stress*, 21, 214–217.

Peterson, C. & Seligman, M. E. P., (2004). *Character Strengths and Virtues: A Handbook Classification*. Washington, DC: American Psychological Association.

Peterson, D. B. (2006). People are complex and the world is messy: A behavior-based approach to executive coaching. In D. R. Stober, & A. M. Grant (Eds.), *Evidence Based Coaching Handbook*, 51-76. New York: Wiley.

Piaget, J. (1970). Piaget's theory. In P. Mussen (Ed.), *Carmichael's Manual of Child Psychology*, 703-732. New York: Wiley.

Plotkin, B. (2003). *Soulcraft: Crossing into the Mysteries of Nature and Psyche*. Novato, CA: New World Library.

Plotkin, B. (2008). *Nature and the Human Soul: Cultivating Wholeness and Community in a Fragmented World*. Novato, CA: New World Library.

Priest, S. (1999) The semantics of adventure programming. In J.C. Miles, & S. Priest (Eds.), *Adventure Programming*. State College, PA: Venture Publishing.

Prochaska, J. O., Norcross, J. C., & DiClemente, C. C. (1995). *Changing for Good*. New York: HarperCollins.

Rogers, C. R. (1951). *Client-Centered Therapy: Its Current Practice, Implications, and Theory*. Boston: Houghton Mifflin.

Rogers, C. R. (1959) A theory of therapy, personality and interpersonal relationships. In S. W. Kochm (Ed.), *Psychology: A Study of Science*, 184-256. New York: McGraw-Hill.

Ryff, C. D. (1989). Happiness is everything, or is it - explorations on the meaning of psychological well-being. *Journal of Personality and Social Psychology, 57*, 1069–1081.

Ryff, C. D., & Singer, B. H. (1996). Psychological well-being: Meaning, measurement, and implications for psychotherapy research. *Psychotherapy and Psychosomatics, 65*, 14–23.

Ryff, C. D., & Singer, B. H. (2003). Ironies of the human condition: Well-being and health on the way to mortality. In Lisa G. Aspinwall & Ursula M. Staudinger (Eds). *A Psychology of Human Strengths: Fundamental Questions and Future Directions for a Positive Psychology*, 271-287. Washington DC: American Psychological Association.

Safran, J. D., & Greenberg, L. S. (Eds.). (1991). *Emotion, Psychotherapy, and Change*. New York: Guilford Press.

Safran, J. D., & Segal, Z. V. (1990). *Interpersonal Process in Cognitive Therapy*. New York: Basic Books.

Sanchez, N., & Vieira, T. (2007). *Take Me to Truth: Undoing the Ego*. Winchester, UK: O Books.

Schatzman, M. (1983). Solve your problems in your sleep. *New Scientist*, 9, 692–693.

Schein, E. H. (1985). *Organizational Culture and Leadership*. San Francisco: Jossey-Bass.

Schneider, S. (2001). In search of realistic optimism. Meaning, knowledge, and warm fuzziness. *American Psychologist*, 56(3), 250-63.

Schwartz, A. J. (2000). The nature of spiritual transformation: A review of the literature. Metanexus Institute, available online at http://www.metanexus.net/spiritual_transformation/research/pdf/STSRP-LiteratureReview2-7.PDF.

Segal, Z. V., Williams, J. M. G., & Teasdale, J. D. (2002). *Mindfulness-Based Cognitive Therapy for Depression: A New Approach to Preventing Relapse*. New York: Guilford Press.

Segers, J., Vloeberghs, D., Henderickx, E., & Inceoglu, I. (2011). Structuring and understanding the coaching Industry: The coaching cube. *Academy of Management Learning & Education*, 10, 204–211.

Seligman, M. E. P. (2002). *Authentic Happiness*. New York: Free Press.

Seligman, M. E. P., Rashid, T., & Parks, A. C. (Nov 2006). Positive psychotherapy. *American Psychologist*, 6(8), 774-788.

Shapiro, D. H. (1994). *Manual for the Shapiro Control Inventory (SCI)*. Palo Alto, CA: Behaviordata.

Shapiro, S. L., Schwartz, G., & Bonner, G. (1998). Effects of mindfulness-based stress reduction on medical and premedical students. *Journal of Behavioral Medicine*, 21, 581-599.

Siegel, D. (1999). *The Developing Mind: How Relationships and the Brain Interact to Shape Who We Are*. New York: Guilford Press.

Siegel, D. (2003). An interpersonal neurobiology of psychotherapy: The developing mind and the resolution of trauma. In M. Solomon & D. J. Siegel (Eds.), *Healing Trauma*, 1-56. New York: W. W. Norton.

Siminovitch, D. E. & Van Eron, A. M. (2006). The pragmatics of magic: The work of Gestalt coaching. *OD Practitioner*, 38(1), 50-55.

Snyder, A. (1995). Executive coaching: The new solution. *Management Review*, 84(3), 29-32.

Snyder, C. R. (Ed.). (2000). *Handbook of Hope: Theory, Measures and Applications*. San Diego, CA: Academic Press.

Sorenson, P., & Yeager, T. (2002). Appreciative inquiry as an approach to organizational consulting. In R. L. Lowman (Ed.), *Handbook of Organizational Consulting* Psychology, 605–616. San Francisco: Jossey-Bass.

Spiegel, D. (1996). Hypnosis in the treatment of post-traumatic stress disorder. *Casebook of Clinical* Hypnosis, 99-112. Washington, DC: American Psychological Association.

Steckler, J. T. (1992). The utilization of hypnosis in psychotherapy: Metaphor and transformation. In M. S. Torem (Ed.), *Psychiatric Medicine: Hypnosis and Its Clinical Applications in Psychiatry and Medicine – I*, 41-50. Longwood, FL: Ryandic Publishing.

Steele, D. (Mar/Apr 2000). Professional coaching and the marriage and family therapist. *The California Therapist*, 54-55.

Steger, M. F., Oishi, S., & Kashdan, T. B. (Jan 2009). Meaning in life across the life span: Levels and correlates of meaning in life from emerging adulthood to older adulthood. *The Journal of Positive Psychology*, 4(1), 43–52.

Stein, S., & Book, H. (2000). *The EQ Edge: Emotional Intelligence and Your Success*. Toronto: MHS.

Stern, D. N. (2004). *The Present Moment in Psychotherapy and Everyday Life.* New York: Norton.

Stober, D. R. (2006). Coaching from the Humanistic Perspective. In D. R. Stober, & A. M. Grant (Eds.), *Evidence Based Coaching Handbook*, 17-50. New York: Wiley.

Stober, D., & Grant, A. M. (2006). Toward a contextual approach to coaching models. In D. R. Stober, & A. M. Grant (Eds.), *Evidence Based Coaching Handbook*, 355-366. New York: Wiley.

Stober, D., Wildflower, L., & Drake, D. (Feb 2006). Evidence-based practice: A potential approach for effective coaching. *International Journal of Evidence-Based Coaching and Mentoring*, 4(1), 1-8.

Sun, B. J., Deane, F. P., Crowe, T. P., Andresen, R., Oades, L., & Ciarrochi, J. (2013). A preliminary exploration of the working alliance and 'real relationship' in two coaching approaches with mental health workers. *International Coaching Psychology Review*, 8(2), 6-17.

Sy, T., Côté, S., & Saavedra, R. (Mar 2005). The contagious leader: Impact of the leader's mood on the mood of group members, group affective tone, and group processes. *Journal of Applied Psychology*, 90(2), 295-305.

Tedeschi, R. G., & Calhoun, L. G. (1995). *Trauma and Transformation: Growing in the Aftermath of Suffering.* Thousand Oaks, CA: Sage.

Tedeschi, R. G., & Calhoun, L. G. (1996). The Posttraumatic Growth Inventory: Measuring the positive legacy of trauma. *Journal of Traumatic Stress*, 9, 455-471.

Tedeschi, R. G., & Calhoun, L. G. (2004). Posttraumatic growth: Conceptual foundations and empirical evidence. *Psychological Inquiry*, 15, 1–18.

Teicher, M. (2000). Wounds time won't heal. *Cerebrum*, 2, 4.

Thinking Allowed - The Rapture of Being with Pir Vilayat Inayat Khan, 1998. Available online at http://www.intuition.org/txt/khan.htm.

Torbert, W. R. (Aug 2002). A conversation with Bill Torbert, July 11, 2002. *Integral Leadership Review*, vol. 2, no. 7. Available online at http://integralleadershipreview.com/archives/2002/2002_08_torbert.html.

Turner, E. (Mar 2010). Coaches' views on the relevance of unconscious dynamics to executive coaching. *Coaching: An International Journal of Theory, Research and Practice*, 3(1), 12-29.

Vieten, C., Amorok, T., & Schlitz, M. (2005). Many paths, one mountain: A cross-traditional model of spiritual transformation. Paper presented at *Science and Religion: Global Perspectives*, sponsored by the Institute of Noetic Sciences and the Metanexus Institute, January 4-8, 2005, in Philadelphia, PA, pp. 4-5.

Vygotsky, L. S. (1978). *Mind in Society: The Development of Higher Psychological Processes.* Cambridge, MA: Harvard University Press.

Wark, D. M. (2006). Alert hypnosis: A review and case report. *American Journal of Clinical Hypnosis*, 48(4), 291–300.

Weick, K. E., & Putnam, T. (2006). Organizing for mindfulness: Eastern wisdom and Western knowledge. *Journal of Management Inquiry*, 15, 275–287.

Westenberg, P. M., & Block, J. (1993). Ego development and individual differences in personality. *Journal of Personality and Social Psychology*, 65, 792-800.

Westin, D. (1998). The Scientific Legacy of Sigmund Freud: Toward a Psychodynamically Informed Psychological Science. *Psychological Bulletin*, 124(3), 333-371.

Winson, J. (Nov 1990). The meaning of dreams. *Scientific American*, 86-96.

Winwood, P. C., Bakker, A. B., & Winefield, A. H. (2007). An investigation of the role of non–work-time behavior in buffering the effects of work strain. *Journal of Occupational and Environmental Medicine*, 49, 862-871.

Yapko, M. (1984). *Trancework: An Introduction to Clinical Hypnosis*. New York: Irvington Press.

Yapko, M. (Sept/Oct 2011). Suggesting mindfulness. *Psychotherapy Networker*, 29-33, 50-52.

Yeager, J. (April 10, 2007). The Digital Scrapbook/Portfolio – Self-Reflection, Savoring and Subjective Well-Being. *Positive Psychology News Daily*. Retrieved from http://positivepsychologynews.com/news/john-yeager/20070410196.

Yi-Ling, L., & McDowall, A. (2014). A systematic review (SR) of coaching psychology: Focusing on the attributes of effective coaching psychologists. *International Coaching Psychology Review*, 9(2), 118-134.

Zahi, A. (2009). Spiritual-transpersonal hypnosis. *Contemporary Hypnosis*, 26(4), 263-268.

Zander, R. S., & Zander, B. (2000). *The Art of Possibility: Transforming Professional and Personal Life*. New York. Penguin Books.

## Endnotes

[1] Ellis, 2006
[2] Seligman et al., 2006
[3] Nelson & Hogan, 2009, p. 15
[4] American Counseling Association, 1997
[5] Maldonado & Spiegel, 1998
[6] Hargrove, 2000
[7] Feltz, Chase, Moritz, & Sullivan, 1999
[8] Maslow, 1971
[9] Metzner, 1980
[10] Maslow, 1968, pp. 71-72
[11] Grant, 2003
[12] Hart, Blattner, & Leipsic, 2001
[13] Caspi, 2005, pp. 360-361
[14] American Psychological Association, 2005
[15] Grove & Panzer, 1989
[16] Frankl, 1960
[17] Pascual-Leone, 1990
[18] Frankl, 1967, p. 9
[19] Crumbaugh & Maholick, 1964
[20] Bion, 1963

[21] de Haan, 2008a, p. 101
[22] de Haan, 2008a, p. 103
[23] Adams & Fitch, 1982
[24] Costa & McCrae, 1994
[25] Kitchener et al., 1984
[26] Erikson, 1963
[27] Erikson, 1969
[28] Jung, 1961
[29] Levinson, 1990
[30] Levinson, 1990, p. 40
[31] Levinson, 1977, p. 99
[32] Levinson, 1990, p. 40
[33] Steger, Oishi, & Kashdan, 2009
[34] Berger, 2006, p. 78
[35] Bauer & McAdams, 2004
[36] Piaget, 1970
[37] Vygotsky, 1978
[38] Freud, 1953
[39] Erikson, 1994
[40] Bowlby, 1969
[41] Maslow, 1968
[42] Loevinger, 1976
[43] Hy & Loevinger, 1996
[44] Ryff, 1989
[45] Bauer & McAdams, 2004, p. 123
[46] Maslow, 1968
[47] Maslow, 1943, p. 382
[48] Maslow, 1971
[49] Jung, 1973, p. 297
[50] Maslow, 1971
[51] Alexander et al., (1990)
[52] Epstein, 1988, p. 62
[53] Engler, 1983, p. 48
[54] Koltko-Rivera, 2006, p. 306
[55] Maslow, 1994
[56] Maslow, 1994, p. 79
[57] Maslow, 1971
[58] Maslow, 1971, p. 281
[59] Maslow, 1996
[60] Maslow, 1996, p. 31

[61] Maslow, 1971b, pp. 270-271.
[62] Hoffman, 1996, p. 206
[63] Maslow, 1971, p. 34
[64] Maslow, 1971, p. 38
[65] Pascual-Leone, 1990
[66] Maslow, 1971b, pp. 273-285
[67] Helson & Roberts, 1994
[68] Westenberg & Block, 1993
[69] Noam, 1998
[70] Westenberg & Block, 1993
[71] Metcalf, 2008
[72] Hatfield & Cacioppo, 1994, pp. 153-154
[73] Sy, Côté, & Saavedra, 2005
[74] Safran & Greenberg, 1991
[75] Masters, 2000
[76] Greenberg, 2002, p. 157
[77] Torbert, 2002
[78] Childre & McCraty, 2001
[79] McCraty, Tiller, & Atkinson, 1996
[80] Siegel, 1999
[81] Siegel, 2003
[82] Shapiro, 1994
[83] Astin et al., 1999
[84] Nelson & Hogan, 2009, p. 7
[85] Sanchez & Vieira, 2007, p. 51
[86] Martin, 1997
[87] Martin, 2002
[88] Deikman, 1982
[89] Safran & Segal, 1990
[90] Langer, 1989
[91] Bohart, 1983
[92] Krishnamurti, 1964
[93] Hick, 2008, p. 5
[94] Kabat-Zinn, 1990
[95] Shapiro, Schwartz, & Bonner,1998
[96] Segal, Williams, & Teasdale, 2002
[97] Vieten, Amorok, & Schlitz, 2005, pp. 4-5
[98] Schwartz, 2000

[99] Carlberg, 1997
[100] Stern, 2004
[101] de Haan, 2008a
[102] de Haan, 2008b
[103] de Haan & Nieß, 2012
[104] Stern, 2004
[105] de Haan, 2008b, p. 106
[106] de Haan, 2008a, p. 104
[107] Scott Asalone, 2010
[108] Hamachek, 1978
[109] Harter, 1999
[110] James, 1890
[111] Bachkirova, 2004
[112] Mayerson, 2013
[113] Aspinwall & Staudinger, 2003
[114] Seligman, 2002
[115] Csikszentmihalyi, 1990
[116] Ryff & Singer, 2003
[117] Hill, 2008
[118] Seligman et al., 2005
[119] Lyubomirsky, Sheldon, & Schkade, 2005
[120] Zander & Zander, 2000
[121] Thinking Allowed, 1998
[122] Findeisen, 1995
[123] Hufford, 2008
[124] Metzner, 1997
[125] Holmes & Rahe, 1967
[126] Hill & Pragament, 2003
[127] American Society of Clinical Hypnosis, 2009
[128] Cox & Ledgerwood, 2003
[129] Hawkins & Smith, 2007
[130] Hawkins & Smith, 2010
[131] Segers et al., 2011
[132] Hawkins & Smith, 2010
[133] Ives, 2008
[134] Stober & Grant, 2006
[135] Rogers, 1951
[136] Rogers, 1959
[137] Peterson, 2006
[138] Berger, 2006

[139] Auerbach, 2006
[140] Ellis, 1979
[141] Burns, 1989
[142] Knowles, 2005
[143] Boud, Cohen, & Walker, 1994
[144] Kolb, 1984
[145] Cox, 2006
[146] Kauffman, 2006
[147] Neenan & Dryden, 2013
[148] Kemp, 2006
[149] Priest, 1999
[150] Cavanagh, 2006
[151] Grant, 2006, p. 153
[152] Grant, 2003
[153] Berg & Szabo, 2005
[154] Grant, 2006, p. 153
[155] Allcorn, 2006
[156] Turner, 2010
[157] Ives, 2008, pp. 103-104
[158] Ives, 2008, pp. 105
[159] Stober & Grant, 2006, p. 3
[160] Snyder, 1995
[161] Stober, Wildflower, & Drake, 2006
[162] Ives, 2008, pp. 107-108
[163] Passmore, 2007
[164] Caruso & Salovey, 2004
[165] Stein & Book, 2000
[166] Stein & Book, 2000
[167] Passmore, 2007, p. 69
[168] de Haan, 2008
[169] de Haan et al., 2011
[170] Yi-Ling & McDowall, 2014
[171] Sun et al., 2013
[172] Biswas-Diener, 2009
[173] American Counseling Association, 1997
[174] Prochaska, Norcross, & DiClemente, 1995
[175] Linley, 2008
[176] Peterson et al., 2008
[177] Seligman, Rashid, & Parks, 2006

[178] Maslow, 1943
[179] Maslow, 1979
[180] McCaslin, 2008
[181] Plotkin, 2003
[182] Plotkin, 2008
[183] Alexander et al., 1990
[184] Pascual-Leone, 1990
[185] Pascual-Leone, 2000
[186] Loevinger, 1976
[187] Bauer, 2008
[188] Cook-Greuter, 2000
[189] Gurdjieff, 1963
[190] Ichazo, 1982
[191] Hartman & Zimberoff, 2008
[192] Grassie, 2007
[193] Pascual-Leone, 1990
[194] Tedeschi & Calhoun, 1995
[195] Tedeschi & Calhoun, 2004
[196] Forgeard, 2013
[197] Janoff–Bulman, 1992
[198] Janoff-Bulman, 2006
[199] Tedeschi & Calhoun, 1996
[200] Joseph & Linley, 2005
[201] Joseph et al., 2012
[202] Ai et al., 2007
[203] Calhoun & Tedeschi, 1999
[204] Tedeschi & Calhoun, 1995
[205] Tedeschi & Calhoun, 2004
[206] Linley & Joseph, 2004
[207] Lechner, Antoni, & Carver, 2006
[208] Levine et al., 2009
[209] Antonovsky, 1987
[210] Antonovsky, 1993
[211] Carver, Scheier, & Weintraub, 1989
[212] Cann et al., 2010
[213] Calhoun, Cann, & Tedeschi, 2010
[214] Park, 2010
[215] Tedeschi & Calhoun, 1995
[216] Janoff-Bulman, 2006

[217] Kobasa, 1979

[218] Maddi & Kobasa, 1984

[219] Maddi, 2006

[220] Hart, Blattner, & Leipsic, 2001, p. 233

[221] Harvey, 2014

[222] Berglas, 2002

[223] Kauffman & Scoular, 2004

[224] Naughton, 2002

[225] British Psychological Society, 2001

[226] Armatas, 2009

[227] Capafons, 2004

[228] Wark, 2006

[229] Bányai, Zseni, & Tury,1997

[230] Armatas, 2009

[231] Palmer, 2008, p. 261

[232] Berger, 2002

[233] Yapko, 2011, p. 31.

[234] Critchley et al., 2004

[235] Barabasz & Barabasz, 2008

[236] Oakley & Halligan, 2010

[237] Winson, 1990

[238] Spiegel, 1996

[239] Larson & Lynch, 1986

[240] Teicher, 2000

[241] de Lange et al., 2008

[242] Corbetta & Shulman, 2002

[243] Buckner & Carroll, 2007

[244] Seeley et al., 2007

[245] Critchley et al., 2004

[246] Barabasz & Barabasz, 2008

[247] Oakley & Halligan, 2010

[248] Winson, 1990

[249] Spiegel, 2008

[250] Maldonado & Spiegel, 1998

[251] Zahi, 2009

[252] Hugdahl, 1996

[253] Lazar et al., 2005

[254] Newberg & Iversen, 2003

[255] Egner, Jamieson, & Gruzelier, 2005

[256] Lutz et al., 2004

[257] Steckler, 1992, pp. 42-44

[258] Yapko, 1984
[259] Bandler & Grinder, 1975
[260] Armatas, 2011
[261] Passmore & Marianetti, 2007
[262] Yeager, 2007
[263] Pelletier, 1979, p. 33
[264] McConkey, 1986
[265] Hornyak, 2004
[266] Brown & Fromm, 1986
[267] Hornyak, 2004
[268] Palmer & Dryden, 1995
[269] Kets de Vries, 2014
[270] Schatzman, 1983
[271] Kets de Vries, 2014, pp. 88-89
[272] Schenk, 2006
[273] Ekman, 2003
[274] Westin, 1998
[275] Kilberg, 2004
[276] Kilberg, 2004, p. 267
[277] Beisser, 1970
[278] Siminovitch & Van Eron, 2006, p. 52
[279] Cooperrider, 1995
[280] Cooperrider et al., 1999
[281] Sorensen & Yeager, 2002
[282] Peterson & Seligman, 2004
[283] Csikszentmihalyi, 1990
[284] Foster & Lloyd, 2007
[285] Lajoie & Shapiro, 1992
[286] Levin, 2009

## Breaking Free from the Victim Trap

*Sixth printing 2013: over 36,000 books in print*

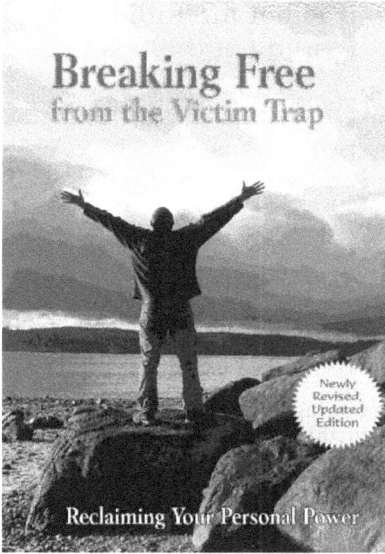

This book has changed the lives of tens of thousands of readers.

It is written clearly and simply, yet carries a profound message of hope. The damage has been done, but the good news is that each of us can repair that damage.

The Victim Game is a family game taught to children in three ways.

The first is by direct example since one or more of the parents is usually a victim in families where this game is played.

Second, the child is programmed by the parent to be a victim.

Third, the victim behavior is reinforced by the parent until it becomes a permanent part of the child's identity.

The child goes through life then having one victim experience after another and each experience reinforces this person's victim position.

The Victim Game can be stopped and changed, but it takes (1) desire to change; (2) awareness; and (3) intensive therapy to change the subconscious programming.

*Discount for quantity orders*.
Call 800-326-4418, or visit the online store at:
**www.wellness-institute.org**

THE WELLNESS INSTITUTE

Now, BREAKING FREE from the VICTIM TRAP
# The <u>Audio</u> Program

**This CD is a companion experience to the book. It is not an audio reading of the book.**

**Discounts for quantity purchases.**

### Track 1
**INTRODUCTION to BREAKING FREE from the VICTIM TRAP**

1. The Law of Attraction
2. Healing through Relationships
3. Addiction to the Drama
4. Reclaiming Personal Power

### Track 2
**HEALING *VICTIM* CONSCIOUSNESS HYPNOTHERAPY EXPERIENCE**

1. Discovering Your Safe Place
2. Identifying Current *Victim* Patterns
3. Discovering the Source of the *Victim*
4. Releasing the Feelings
5. Nurturing the Inner Child
6. Creating a New Healthy Pattern
7. Empowerment Affirmations

### Track 3
**HEALING VICTIM CONSCIOUSNESS**
*Beautiful Butterfly* (Bobbi Branch)

### Track 4
**HEALING *RESCUER* CONSCIOUSNESS HYPNOTHERAPY EXPERIENCE**

1. Discovering Your Safe Place
2. Identifying Current *Rescuer* Patterns
3. Discovering the Source of the *Rescuer*
4. Releasing the Feelings
5. Nurturing the Inner Child
6. Creating a New Healthy Pattern
7. Empowerment Affirmations

### Track 5
**HEALING RESCUER CONSCIOUSNESS**
*Sing Your Own Song* (Bobbi Branch)

### Track 6
**HEALING *PERSECUTOR* CONSCIOUSNESS HYPNOTHERAPY EXPERIENCE**

1. Discovering Your Safe Place
2. Identifying Current *Persecutor* Patterns
3. Discovering the Source of the *Persecutor*
4. Releasing the Feelings
5. Nurturing the Inner Child
6. Creating a New Healthy Pattern
7. Empowerment Affirmations

THE WELLNESS INSTITUTE

# OVERCOMING SHOCK

## Healing the Traumatized Mind and Heart

DIANE ZIMBEROFF, LMFT
& DAVID HARTMAN, LICSW

# Overcoming Shock: Healing the Traumatized Mind and Heart

### By Diane Zimberoff & David Hartman

*newly published in 2014*

What is shock? It is a physiological response to any distress that seems intolerable and in which I feel intensely helpless. It is the body saying, "I can't deal with this right now, I need a moment to collect myself." And in the case of a car accident, for example, the person "comes back" after a brief time. But an individual who is consistently in shock can't take that moment, they must find a way to keep going despite the disruption, to live their life in shock. This would be a soldier in a combat zone, a family in the aftermath of a natural disaster or terrorist attack, or a child in an abusive home. Here the assault is on the person's psyche itself, and that abuses their spirit, damages their self esteem, and undermines their courage to "come back" from the protective numbness of shock. And so these individuals develop ways of living their life, doing what needs to be done, in spite of the handicap of constantly being in a state of shock. Here we address how to recognize shock and how to heal it.

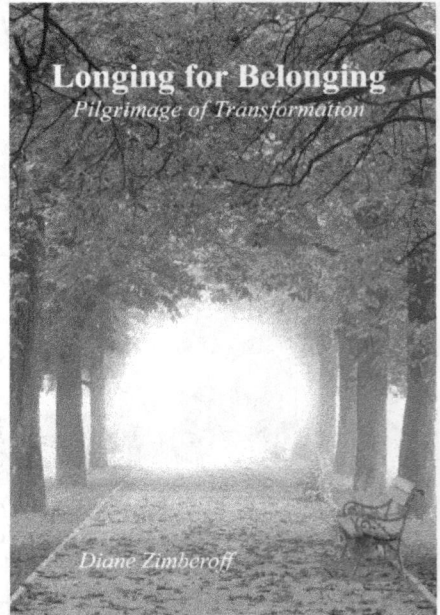

# Collecting Lessons: A Fable

**By David Hartman**

*newly published in 2007*

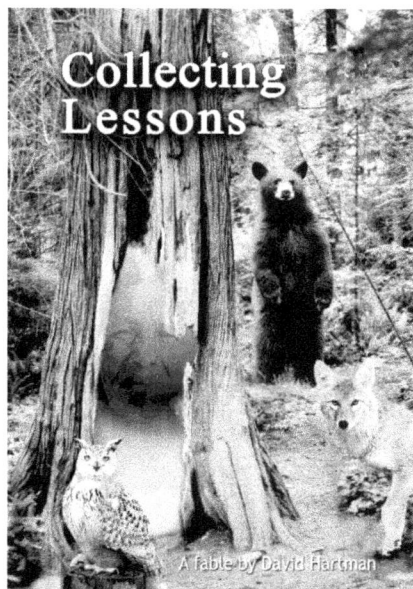

This book offers an intriguing story told by a compelling storyteller. It combines folklore, fairy tales, appreciation for our interdependence with nature, state-of-the-art trauma neuroscience, and ancient wisdom (Buddhist, Kabbalah, Tarot, Sufi, and Perennial Wisdom) in a playful, entertaining format: a fable in the tradition of Carlos Castaneda's recounting of *The Teachings of Don Juan* or Aesop's wisdom tales. The story presents practical life lessons to ease the reader through six stages of spiritual unfoldment. In this book the teachings come directly from power animals, and will inspire the reader to discover steps on their own practical path toward fulfillment. The ideas presented are carefully annotated in extensive endnotes for those who want sources.

# The Chakras Meditation
## 2 CD set

### FIRST CD
### Track 1
### INTRODUCTION TO MEDITATION

1. Creating Sacred Space
2. Benefits of Chakra Meditation
3. Quieting the Mind
4. Receiving a Spiritual Mantra

### Track 2
### ACTIVATING LOWER CHAKRAS

1. Connecting with the Earth
2. Power Animal's Message
3. Cleansing the Chakras
4. Release Energetic Drains
5. Connecting with Divine Presence

### Track 3
### ACTIVATING HIGHER CHAKRAS

1. Cleansing the Higher Chakras
2. Heart Space above the Head
3. Compassion for Humanity
4. Soul Retrieval
5. Aura Expansion & Healing Energy

### SECOND CD
### Track 1
### SOUL RETRIEVAL MEDITATION

1. Discovering Soul-splits in each Chakra
2. Cleansing Soul Fragments
3. Reclaiming Soul Fragments
4. Hearing your Soul's Message
5. Embracing the Symbol in each Chakra
6. Sealing the Soul in each Chakra

### Track 2
### MIND - BODY - SPIRIT HEALING

1. Pranayama Breathing
2. Discovering the Glands, Hormones and Organs in each Chakra
3. Manifesting Healing in each Chakra
4. Affirmations for Mind-Body Healing
5. Focusing on specific areas for Increased Healing
6. Calling in your Healing Angels

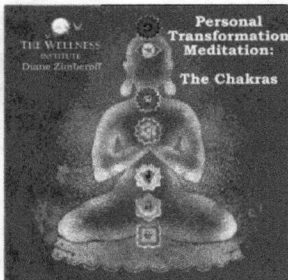

Personal Transformation Meditation: The Chakras — THE WELLNESS INSTITUTE Diane Zimberoff

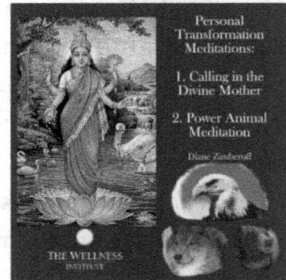

Personal Transformation Meditations: 1. Calling in the Divine Mother 2. Power Animal Meditation — Diane Zimberoff — THE WELLNESS INSTITUTE

# Divine Mother and Power Animal Meditations

### Track 1
### CALLING IN THE DIVINE MOTHER

1. The Root Chakra - Lakshmi
2. The Sacral Chakra - Shakti
3. The Solar Plexus Chakra - Kali
4. The Heart Chakra - Durga
5. The Throat Chakra - Saraswati
6. The Third Eye Chakra - Parvati
7. The Crown Chakra – Narayani/Ishwari

### Track 2
### POWER ANIMAL MEDITATION

Discovering the Power Animal in each Chakra

Finding the individual message carried by each animal for your healing and personal growth

# Personal Transformation Intensive
## PTI

This is a profoundly healing group process, meeting for five weekend retreats over five months, in a loving environment. Do you long for these changes in your life?

## Attract Healthy, Loving, Fulfilling Relationships
Belong to a new healthy, high-powered family • Develop close in-depth friendships instead of "cocktail party superficial phoniness" • Learn healthy support (not competition) • Learn to love yourself so you can love others

## Experience Personal Growth and Transformation
Self-awareness • Higher consciousness • Self-discovery

## Manifest Your Goals using the full power of your mind:
It's time to stop wanting things to happen in your life and time to start making things happen • Learn to use 100% of your mind to reach your full potential with a new goal-setting process • Discover your unconscious goals • Get clear on what you want • Become a member of a Master Mind Group

## Improved Health with Powerful Stress Reduction Tools
Learn messages that your body is telling you • Release body hatred and shame • Relaxation Anchors • Heart-centered meditation • Conscious Breathing

## Improved Finances
Prosperity and abundance principles • Master Mind groups • Learn the role of integrity in creating your abundance

## Release Self -Defeating Patterns
Procrastination • "Victim, Rescuer, Persecutor" • Fear-based decisions (learn to make clear decisions) • Codependency • Unhealthy relationship patterns

## Improved Communication Skills
Learn "The Clearing Process" • Stop "The Blame Game"

## Take Full Responsibility for your Life!
Stop sabotaging yourself • Learn accountability and integrity • Release the shame which diminishes your self-esteem • Release self-judgment, self-blame

THE WELLNESS INSTITUTE
800-326-4418

# Journal of Heart-Centered Therapies

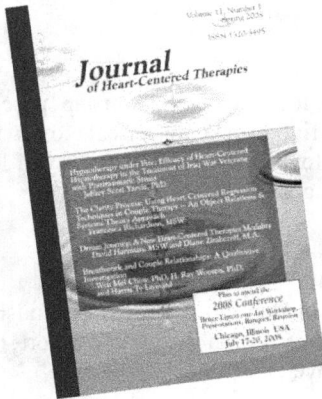

Selected articles
APPROVED
for
Distance CE credit
(5 hours each)

## APPROVALS:

### Social Workers

The Wellness Institute is approved as a provider for distance continuing education by The National Association of Social Workers (NASW) to offer 5 hours of credit for selected Journal articles (provider # 886422919).

### Professional Counselors

The Wellness Institute is recognized by the National Board of Certified Counselors to offer continuing education for certified counselors. We adhere to NBCC continuing education guidelines. Provider #5460 (5 hours of credit for selected Journal articles).

There are test questions and a fee of $50 per 5 hours of CE.

## The Heart-Centered Therapies Association
3716 - 274th Ave SE, Issaquah, WA  98029  ❖  425-391-9716  ❖  800-326-4418

# Index of Back Issues of the Journal

# The Heart-Centered Therapies Association

3716 - 274th Avenue SE, Issaquah, WA 98029 USA ❖ 425-391-9716 ❖ 800-326-4418

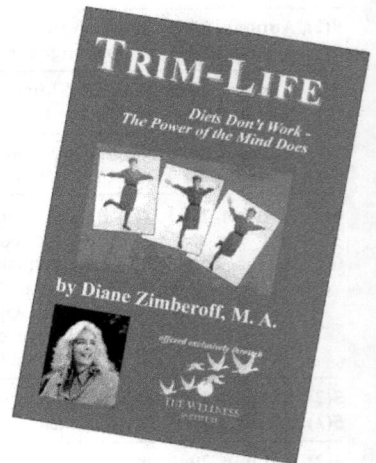

www.ingramcontent.com/pod-product-compliance
Lightning Source LLC
Chambersburg PA
CBHW072013290326
41934CB00007BA/1073